ABS OF STEEL, BUNS OF CINNAMON

Other Cathy® Books from Andrews McMeel Publishing

Understanding the "Why" Chromosome
The Child Within Has Been Awakened But the Old Lady on the Outside Just Collapsed
Revelations from a 45-Pound Purse
Only Love Can Break a Heart, But a Shoe Sale Can Come Close
$14 in the Bank and a $200 Face in My Purse
My Granddaughter Has Fleas!!
Why Do the Right Words Always Come out of the Wrong Mouth?
A Hand to Hold, an Opinion to Reject
Thin Thighs in Thirty Years
Wake Me Up When I'm a Size 5
Men Should Come with Instruction Booklets
A Mouthful of Breath Mints and No One to Kiss
Another Saturday Night of Wild and Reckless Abandon

Cathy Twentieth Anniversary Collection
Reflections: A Fifteenth Anniversary Collection

ABS OF STEEL, BUNS OF CINNAMON

A Cathy® COLLECTION BY CATHY GUISEWITE

Andrews McMeel Publishing

Kansas City

Cathy® is distributed internationally by Universal Press Syndicate.

www.andrewsmcmeel.com

ISBN: 0-8362-3683-1

Library of Congress Catalog Card Number: 97-71622

Cathy® may be viewed on the Internet at:
www.uexpress.com

ANOTHER NEW GYM HERE... ANOTHER NEW GOURMET BAKERY THERE...

GYM

A STORE FULL OF EXERCISE EQUIPMENT HERE... A STORE FULL OF GIANT MUFFINS THERE...

FITNESS

FROM TWO POWERFUL TRENDS, ONE AWESOME NEW SILHOUETTE...

ABS OF STEEL, BUNS OF CINNAMON.

BAKERY

Guisewite

WHEN CATHY COMES HOME FOR CHRISTMAS, I WILL TREAT HER AS A MATURE ADULT!

NO MORE PICKING. NO HOVERING. NO NAGGING ABOUT THINGS THAT ARE NONE OF MY BUSINESS. AFTER ALL THESE YEARS, I'M FINALLY READY TO WELCOME THE INDEPENDENT, SELF-RELIANT WOMAN SHE IS!

FEED ME, MOM! WASH MY CLOTHES! FLUFF UP MY BED! MAKE ME TAKE MY VITAMINS! TELL ME WHAT TO DO WITH MY STUPID LIFE!

FOR THE MILLIONTH TIME IN A ROW, I'M COMPLETELY READY TO COPE WITH THE PHASE SHE JUST MOVED OUT OF...
Guisewite

THANKS AGAIN, CATHY.
...OH, NO. I JUST THOUGHT OF THE PERFECT GIFT TO GIVE HIM...
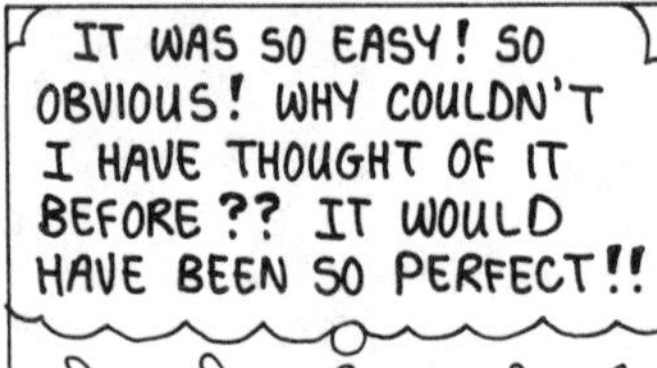
IT WAS SO EASY! SO OBVIOUS! WHY COULDN'T I HAVE THOUGHT OF IT BEFORE?? IT WOULD HAVE BEEN SO PERFECT!!

WAIT! COME BACK! GIVE ME BACK WHAT I JUST GAVE YOU!! I FINALLY HAVE THE PERFECT IDEA!!

FOR ONCE IN MY LIFE, THE GIFT WAS ON TIME, BUT NOW THE INSPIRATION IS BELATED.
Guisewite

THE MEYERS ARE SPENDING THE WEEK MAKING LITTLE DOLL HOUSE REPLICAS OF THEIR HOME FOR EACH OF THEIR NINE VISITING GRANDCHILDREN.

THE CROWLEYS RENTED A SKI CHALET IN SWITZERLAND FOR THE HOLIDAYS FOR A REUNION WITH ALL THEIR EUROPEAN RELATIVES.

IT'S 10:00AM, AND WE'VE ALREADY EATEN THREE MEALS!

EVERY FAMILY HAS A REASON TO BE PROUD.
Guisewite

OH, GOODNESS. WE CAN'T PUT THIS ONE IN THE ALBUM! MY LIPSTICK'S ON CROOKED!
THIS ONE CAN'T GO IN THE ALBUM! MY REAR LOOKS HUGE!

MY HAIR LOOKS LIKE IT'S THINNING IN THIS ONE.
MY DRESS IS TOO BUNCHY IN THIS ONE.
I LOOK LIKE A GEEK IN THIS ONE.

BAD SHAVE.
BAD HAIR.
BAD SMILE.
BAD SOCKS.
BAD LEGS.
BAD ANGLE.

OUR FAMILY PHOTO SYSTEM: 25 BLANK ALBUMS IN THE DEN, AND A BASEMENT FULL OF OUTTAKES.
PHOTOS
Guisewite

FLO MUST HAVE BEEN UP ALL NIGHT MAKING THAT HORS D'OEUVRES PLATTER!!
...AND WHAT ABOUT THAT CHOCOLATE CHEESECAKE AT AUNT RENA'S??

IT WAS WORTH THE HALF-HOUR DRIVE TO THE WILSON'S OPEN HOUSE FOR A TASTE OF THAT CARAMEL PUDDING!
MY FAVORITE IS STILL THOSE POWDERED SUGAR BALLS AT THE JACOBS'!

WHEW! WHAT A WEEK!
HA, HA! WHAT A WEEK!!

MAY I HELP YOU?
YES. WE'D LIKE TO KEEP THE GIFTS, BUT RETURN THE TEN POUNDS OF CELEBRATORY FAT.
RETURNS
Guisewite

HERE, SWEETIE! WHY DON'T YOU POLISH OFF THIS LITTLE DAB OF CAKE BEFORE YOU GO?

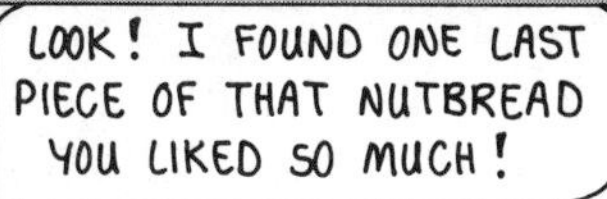

LOOK! I FOUND ONE LAST PIECE OF THAT NUTBREAD YOU LIKED SO MUCH!

OOPS! HALF A TIN OF FROSTED SANTAS! DON'T FORGET THE FROSTED SANTAS!

CATHY WON'T LET ME NEAR HER SUITCASE, SO I'M HELPING HER PACK HER STOMACH.
Guisewite

I HAVE THE DATE. I HAVE THE SLINKY GOWN. I HAVE THE HEELS, THE EARRINGS, THE SPARKLE, THE ATTITUDE, THE HAIR, THE SHAWL...

FOR ONCE IN MY LIFE, IT'S NEW YEAR'S EVE, AND I HAVE IT ALL!!!

OH, BY THE WAY, CATHY, DID I MENTION IT'S JUST CASUAL TONIGHT?

THE YEAR ENDS AS IT BEGAN...STANDING IN THE LADIES' ROOM, DRAPED IN FANTASIES AND CLUTCHING A LITTLE EVENING BAG.
Guisewite

HI, JIM. HOW'S IT GOING?
STUFFY NOSE, ACHY MUSCLES.
RECEPTION

HI, JOYCE. HOW ARE YOU DOING?
CLOGGED BREATHING PASSAGES, RAW THROAT, WATERY EYES.
RECEPTION

HI, GEORGE. WHAT'S NEW?
FEVER. CHILLS. BRAIN-NUMBING CONGESTION. HOARSE VOICE. ACHING CHEST. MILD HALLUCI-NATIONS.
RECEPTION

HELLO. HEALTH CARE GROUP #Q429XPIK28 WOULD LIKE OUR MONEY BACK FOR OUR FLU SHOTS!
SORRY. ALL AGENTS ARE OUT SICK TODAY.
Guisewite

...AND THEN, cough ..OOPS. SORRY. I HAD A LITTLE SCRATCH IN MY THROAT.
UH, OH. THAT'S JUST HOW MINE STARTED.

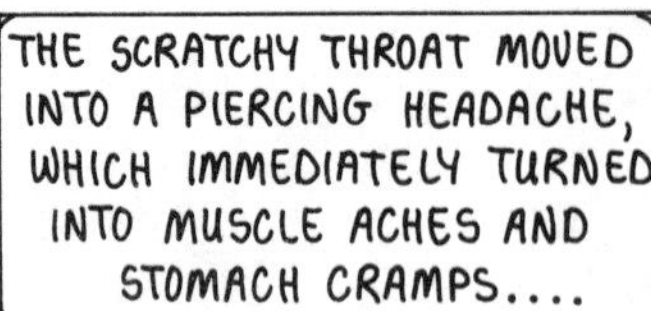
THE SCRATCHY THROAT MOVED INTO A PIERCING HEADACHE, WHICH IMMEDIATELY TURNED INTO MUSCLE ACHES AND STOMACH CRAMPS....

WITHIN SIX HOURS, I'D COL-LAPSED INTO A CLAMMY, WHEEZING HEAP, UNABLE TO LIFT A SPOON OF CHICKEN BROTH TO MY LIPS! WHEW! ARE YOU IN FOR A NIGHTMARE!

FLU SEASON, '95: WHAT THE GERMS DON'T GET, THE AIRBORNE COMMISERA-TION MOLECULES WILL.
Guisewite

OH, NO. YOU'RE SICK TOO, CATHY?
PHIL GOT SICK FIRST. JULIE MUST HAVE PICKED UP THE GERMS FROM HIS DESK.

JULIE PASSED THEM ON TO MARGO, WHO PASSED THEM ON TO JOHN, WHO SPREAD THEM THROUGH ACCOUNTING...

...WHO TOOK THEM TO STAN IN LEGAL, WHO HANDED THEM OUT TO EVERYONE ELSE WITH THE POPCORN IN THE STAFF MEETING.

DO WE CURSE THE GERMS, OR APPLAUD THE FACT THAT SOMETHING FINALLY MADE IT THROUGH THE INTER-OFFICE ROUTING SYSTEM?

I FEEL TERRIBLE. I HAVE TO GO HOME AND LIE DOWN!
LIE DOWN? HAH!

AS SOON AS YOU LIE DOWN, THE GERMS SPREAD OUT ALL OVER YOU! YOU HAVE TO STAY VERTICAL! ATTACK BACK!

THROW DOWN SOME MEGA-VITAMINS! CRUSH THE COOTIES WITH YOUR WILL! THEN TAKE WHATEVER'S LEFT OF YOUR LITTLE COLD AND SWEAT IT OFF ON THE TREADMILL!!

GOODBYE, OLD WIVES' TALES. HELLO, NEW HUSBANDS' TALES.
...OH, NO! MY NOSE IS DRIPPING! ORDER ME SOME ANTIBIOTICS!!

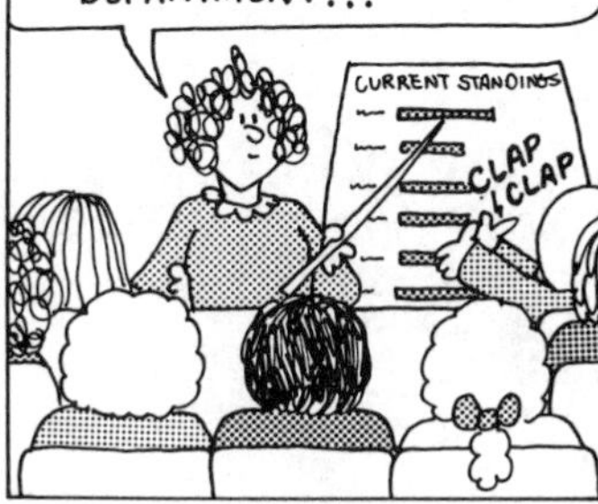
AND NOW FOR TODAY'S SCORECARD: THE FLU STRAIN THAT BRIAN'S SON BROUGHT HOME FROM PRESCHOOL HAS FLATTENED HALF THE ACCOUNTING DEPARTMENT...
CLAP CLAP

...WHILE THE SINUS INFECTION BEGUN AT KAREN'S DAUGHTER'S DAY CARE HAS CLAIMED SIX OUT OF NINE NOSES IN DATA PROCESSING.
CLAP CLAP

HOWEVER, LEADING THE GERM PLAYOFFS IS STILL THE STREP THROAT THAT SAM'S TWINS CARRIED HOME FROM KINDERGARTEN, WHICH HAS SILENCED THE ENTIRE MANAGEMENT SQUAD!

CAN'T YOU PEOPLE GET YOUR CHILDREN INTO TEAM SPORTS OR SOMETHING IN THE WINTER??
FRANK'S DAUGHTER'S SOCCER TEAM NAILED THE MAILROOM WITH CHICKEN POX.

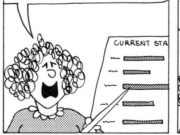

YOU WENT TO EVERYONE IN YOUR OFFICE FOR THEIR FLU REMEDIES... YOU BEGGED FOUR DOCTORS FOR A CURE...
Tissues
FLU RELAX

YOU EVEN CALLED YOUR BOY-FRIEND FOR HIS CHICKEN SOUP RECIPE!
Tissues
FLU RELAX

YOU'VE ASKED EVERYONE TO BE YOUR MOTHER EXCEPT ME! WHAT DOES THAT MAKE ME??
OH, YOU'LL ALWAYS BE MY MOTHER, MOM... I JUST THOUGHT SOMEONE ELSE WOULD HAVE A BETTER SUGGESTION.

ONCE AGAIN, I'VE BEEN LEFT OUT OF MY OWN LOOP.
Guisewite

I FEEL TERRIBLE.
YOU DON'T LOOK SICK ANYMORE, CATHY.
BUT I FEEL TERRIBLE.
BUT YOU DON'T LOOK SICK AT ALL ANYMORE.

LADIES

SCRUB
SCRUB
SCRUB
SOAP

AACK! YOU LOOK TERRIBLE! GO HOME!
MORE POWER-FUL THAN THE FLU VIRUS: THE FRESH, DEWY, NO MAKEUP LOOK.
Guisewite

TO DO TODAY:
* CHEW BOOTS
* DIG UP PLANT IN LIVING ROOM
* PRACTICE OPENING SNACK CUPBOARD WITH NOSE
* SHRED PANTYHOSE
* FINISH EATING WOODWORK AT BASE OF DOORS
* GRIND FLEAS INTO SOFA
* TRY TO PERFECT MORE EAR-PIERCING BARK
* DROOL ON ALL UPHOL-STERED FURNITURE
FIDOFAX

I'M STILL TOO SICK TO GO BACK TO THE OFFICE, ELECTRA...

...BUT AT LEAST I'LL GET TO WATCH WHAT YOU DO ALL DAY WHEN I'M GONE.
ONE BOUT WITH THE FLU, AND MY SCHEDULE IS SET BACK A MONTH.
Guisewite

FOUNDATION TO COVER THE RED, DRIPPING NOSE... SMOLDERING SHADOW TO DISGUISE THE PUFFY, BLOOD-SHOT EYES....

...WHAT AM I DOING?? WHAT CRUEL FEMALE GENE MAKES ME THINK THAT EVEN IN ILLNESS I'M SUPPOSED TO BE ALLURING?? HAH!

I REJECT THE STEREOTYPE! I REFUSE TO PERPETUATE THE MYTH! I CLAIM MY RIGHT TO LOOK EXACTLY AS BAD AS I.....

I BROUGHT THE SOUP, CATHY!
THE CURSE OF MY AGE BRACKET... ...YOUNG ENOUGH TO KNOW BETTER, BUT OLD ENOUGH TO NEED A TOUCH OF LIPSTICK...

WHAT'S WRONG WITH YOUR FACE, ALEX?
I'M WEARING A SURGICAL MASK AND GLOVES TO PROTECT MYSELF FROM YOUR FLU GERMS, CATHY.

I KNOW LOTS OF MEN ARE TOO MACHO TO WORRY ABOUT AN AIRBORNE VIRUS... BUT THEN, THOSE MEN WOULDN'T HAVE TAKEN THE AFTERNOON OFF TO COOK YOU A POT OF SOUP.

YOU CAN HAVE ME HERE, THE EMBODIMENT OF PHYSICAL AND EMOTIONAL HEALTH... ...OR YOU CAN HAVE A TOUGH GUY ON THE PHONE WHO TELLS YOU TO CALL WHEN YOU'VE COMPLETELY RECOVERED.

MUST YOU BE SO STRAIGHT-FORWARD??!
FOR MYSTERY, YOU NEED TYPE "C"... ...BUT THEN, HE WOULD HAVE LEFT TOWN AT THE FIRST SIGN OF A SNIFFLE.

"I CAN'T AFFORD ANOTHER DAY OFF WORK", 1975:
PAPERS ARE PILING UP AT THE OFFICE. WHATEVER WILL I DO???

"I CAN'T AFFORD ANOTHER DAY OFF WORK", 1995:
HELLO! SEND ME THE DANGLING CUBIC ZIRCONIA EARRINGS, THE MAGENTA LOUNGE-WEAR ENSEMBLE, THE COMMEMORA-TIVE PLATE, THE MINIATURE REPLICA OF GRACELAND AND THE 27-PIECE CRYSTAL BELL SET WITH DISPLAY STAND!

I HAVE RECOVERED FROM THE FLU AND VOW TO TAKE BETTER CARE OF MYSELF FROM THIS MOMENT ON!
RECEPT

I WILL ELIMINATE STRESS! I WILL TAKE TIME FOR RELAXING, NUTRITIOUS MEALS! I WILL RELEASE ALL NEGATIVE ENERGY AND TENSION THROUGH THE SIMPLE, HEALTHY, HEALING POWER OF LAUGHTER!!

CATHY'S BACK??!!?
RECEPTION

HA, HA.

HEY! YOU CAN'T TAKE CUTS! THE LINE TO GET ON THE FREEWAY STARTS A MILE BACK THERE! NO CUTS!
HONK
HONK
HONK

LET ME CHANGE LANES! LET ME CHANGE... AACK! GET OFF THE PHONE! YOU ALMOST REAR-ENDED ME!
HONK HONK

USE YOUR TURN SIGNAL, YOU MORON!... YELLOW MEANS SLOW DOWN, NOT HURRY UP!... PUT DOWN THAT BURRITO! THIS ISN'T A CAFETERIA!!
HONK
HONK
HONK

YOU LOOK AWFUL, CATHY!
THE DRIVERS WERE SO TERRIBLE THIS MORNING, I ONLY HAD TIME TO PUT ON HALF OF MY MAKEUP.
RECEPTION

NICE EYES. GOOD HAIR. GREAT BRAIN. FABULOUS SPIRIT.

LOVING NATURE. SOLID VALUE SYSTEM. FINE SENSE OF HUMOR. GOOD ATTITUDE. DECENT JOB. COMFORTABLE HOME.

AS THE SUN SETS ON ANOTHER DAY, THE CLASSIC '90s COUPLE SNUGGLES IN FOR THE EVENING...

MISS RIGHT AND MR. REFRIGERATOR.
TV GUIDE

I'M ON THE ALL-NEW, NOT-THINKING-ABOUT-IT DIET, CHARLENE!
AS SOON AS I THINK ABOUT IT, THE FAT CELLS BRACE FOR A FIGHT, THE APPETITE INCREASES FOR BATTLE, AND I'M DOOMED.
AS LONG AS I DON'T THINK ABOUT IT, THERE'S NO TRAUMA-INDUCED EATING... ...NO CELLULITE-MULTIPLYING ANGST...I SIMPLY HAVE NICE, NORMAL MEALS WHEN I'M HUNGRY, AND THAT'S THAT!
HOW ARE YOU DOING SO FAR?
UP TWO AND A HALF POUNDS.
BRAVO! ON A NORMAL DIET, YOU WOULD HAVE GAINED FOUR BY NOW!
Guisewite

TO DO
MAKE:
* HAIR APPOINTMENT
* DENTIST APPOINTMENT
* EYE APPOINTMENT
* DERMATOLOGIST APPOINTMENT
* MAMMOGRAM APPOINTMENT
* VETERINARIAN APPOINTMENT
* CAR TUNE-UP APPOINTMENT

ARRANGE TO MEET:
*PLUMBER AT HOUSE
*ELECTRICIAN AT HOUSE
*CABLE COMPANY AT HOUSE
*PHONE COMPANY AT HOUSE
*HEATING COMPANY AT HOUSE
* CARPENTER AT HOUSE
* RUG CLEANER AT HOUSE

REPLACE:
*BROKEN TV
*BROKEN STEREO
*BROKEN VCR
*BROKEN PHONE
*BROKEN HAIRDRYER
*BROKEN COFFEE MAKER
*BROKEN VACUUM
*BROKEN GARBAGE DISPOSAL

I'M NOW SUPPORTING HALF THE CITY. HOWEVER, I NO LONGER HAVE TIME TO GO TO MY JOB.
Guisewite

SIMON SAID WE NEEDED TO TALK...
OH, NO. DON'T SAY IT, CHARLENE!

...AND THE NEXT THING YOU KNOW, WE'RE YELLING AND...
EVERY TIME YOU TALK ABOUT **YOUR** RELATIONSHIP PROBLEMS, THEY BECOME **MY** RELATIONSHIP PROBLEMS!

I DON'T WANT MY AIR POLLUTED WITH YOUR PSYCHODRAMA! I REFUSE TO BREATHE YOUR BAD VIBES! **I'M NOT LISTENING! NOT BREATHING! NOT....**

RING RING

HI, CATHY. IT'S ALEX. WE NEED TO TALK.
..ONCE AGAIN, NAILED BY EMOTIONAL SECONDHAND SMOKE.
Guisewite

ALEX SAID WE NEED TO TALK.
UH, OH. TROUBLE.

MAYBE HE WANTS TO TALK ABOUT SOMETHING GOOD.
NO. "**I WANT TO TALK**" COULD BE SOMETHING GOOD...."**LET'S TALK**" COULD BE SOMETHING GOOD...

...EVEN "**I NEED TO TALK**" COULD BE SOMETHING GOOD... ...BUT "**WE NEED TO TALK**" CAN ONLY MEAN SOMETHING REALLY HIDEOUS. SORRY.

I FINALLY MET A MAN WHO USED "WE" IN A SENTENCE, AND HE USED IT IN THE WRONG ONE.
Guisewite

—1984—
WHIMPERED, WHINED AND WEPT UNTIL I GOT A VALENTINE.

JUST ONCE, I WANT TO BE SWEPT OFF MY FEET WHEN I'M NOT THE ONE HOLDING THE BROOM.
DIARY
diet
Guisewite

WHY SHOULD I WORRY ABOUT WHAT TO GET ALEX FOR VALENTINE'S DAY ? WHATEVER HAPPENED TO THE GOOD OLD DAYS OF "WOMAN AS PASSIVE RECIPIENT" ??

WHAT HAPPENED TO BEING COURTED?? WHAT HAPPENED TO SITTING BACK UNDER A PARASOL AND GRANTING SOMEONE A CHANCE TO TRY TO WIN US OVER??!

WE OPTED FOR RESPECT, SELF-ESTEEM, EQUALITY AND MUTUALLY INVOLVED PARTNERSHIPS... REMEMBER?

CATHY'S HAVING HER ANNUAL PRE-VALENTINE'S DAY REGRESSION.
WHAT WERE WE THINKING?? MEN EVEN PREFERRED US PLUMP BACK THEN!
DONUTS
Guisewite

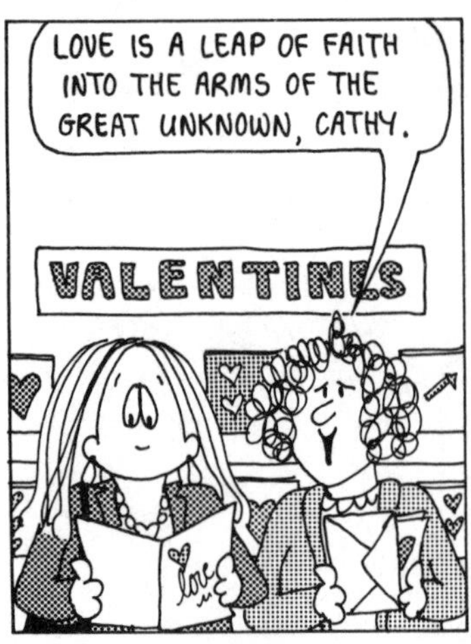
LOVE IS A LEAP OF FAITH INTO THE ARMS OF THE GREAT UNKNOWN, CATHY.
VALENTINES
love

TO EXPERIENCE ANYTHING, YOU HAVE TO RISK EVERYTHING.
VALENTINES
love

YOU HAVE TO OPEN YOUR HEART, MIND AND SOUL, AND LET YOURSELF BE COMPLETELY, UTTERLY VULNERABLE TO THE DEEPEST FEELINGS OF LIFE!
love

WHAT IF I GET TRAMPLED IN THE PROCESS?
THEN YOU JOIN A SUPPORT GROUP, WHERE YOU DO THE SAME THING, EXCEPT YOU DON'T HAVE TO WEAR MAKEUP.
Guisewite

20 ACRES OF VALENTINE GIFTS, AND THE ONLY PEOPLE WHO SEE THEM ARE WOMEN BECAUSE MEN DON'T GO SHOPPING.

VALENTINES
FOR HER
FOR HER
FOR HER

20 ACRES OF GIFTS, ALL SCREAMING THAT SOME OTHER WOMAN HAS THE KIND OF RELATIONSHIP WHERE, SAY, A DIAMOND BROOCH IS APPROPRIATE... 20 ACRES OF GIFTS THAT SIMULTANEOUSLY RAISE THE EXPECTATIONS AND TRAMPLE THE SPIRIT OF THE FEMALE POPULATION....

For Her

FOR HER
FOR HER
FOR HER
FOR HER
FOR HER

BAN THE VALENTINE DISPLAYS!!
BUS THE MEN TO THE MALLS!!
Guisewite

I HAVE TO EAT LOTS OF CHOCOLATE TODAY JUST IN CASE ALEX GIVES ME A BOX TOMORROW.
DITTO.

IF I SATURATE MY CELLS WITH CHOCOLATE TODAY, I WON'T HUMILIATE MYSELF BY DIVING INTO THE GIFT BOX, AS I HAVE ON OTHER OCCASIONS.
DITTO.

I WILL EAT AND BREATHE CHOCOLATE UNTIL IT LOSES ITS POWER OVER ME AND I CAN RECEIVE MY VALENTINE IN A DEMURE AND DIGNIFIED MANNER!

WE'RE NOT PIGGING OUT. WE'RE DESENSITIZING OURSELVES.
PASS THE FUDGE CREAMS. I STILL FEEL A LITTLE SOMETHING.

WHAT ???
OH, I KNOW ABOUT THE AGE DIFFERENCE, THE INTEREST DIFFERENCE, THE LIFESTYLE DIFFERENCE, THE "YOU'RE READY FOR KIDS AND I'M NOT" DIFFERENCE...
...BUT **EVERYONE'S** GETTING MARRIED, CATHY!!

I MEAN, **WHY NOT**?? LET'S GET MOVING! GET ON WITH IT! GO FOR IT! GO THE DISTANCE!

RAISED ON THE POETRY OF THE ATHLETIC SHOE AD, THE FITNESS GENERATION DELIVERS A VALENTINE THAT DEFINES THE DECADE...

...THE ACTIVE-WEAR PROPOSAL.
WHAT ???
JUST DO IT! MARRY ME! JUST DO IT!!

RING!...**BEEP**... HI, CATHY, IT'S ALEX. YOU HAVEN'T ANSWERED YOUR PHONE SINCE I PROPOSED LAST NIGHT. WHERE ARE YOU?

RING!...**BEEP**... HI, CATHY, IT'S CHARLENE. WHY AREN'T YOU AT THE OFFICE? ARE YOU OK? WHERE ARE YOU?

RING!...**BEEP**... HI, CATHY, IT'S MOM. WHAT'S GOING ON? I HAVEN'T HEARD FROM YOU. WHERE ARE YOU?

AFTER A LIFETIME OF WAITING FOR HER SHIP TO COME IN, ANOTHER WOMAN SITS PARALYZED ON THE DOCK.

I'VE BEEN TRYING TO CALL YOU FOR TWO DAYS, CATHY! I'VE LEFT A DOZEN MESSAGES! I'VE BEEN WORRIED SICK!

THERE'S NO EXCUSE TO NOT PICK UP THE PHONE AND...

AACK!!

RING!...BEEP...HI, CATHY, IT'S DAD. IS MOM THERE? WHERE ARE YOU??

WHY DID YOU GET SO WEIRD, CATHY?? I ONLY ASKED YOU TO MARRY ME.
JAVA HOUSE

IF IT DOESN'T WORK OUT, WE'LL GET DIVORCED. WHAT'S THE BIG DEAL? HALF THE PEOPLE I KNOW ARE DIVORCED.

LOTS OF MY FRIENDS LOOK AT THE FIRST MARRIAGE AS A TRIAL RUN, ANYWAY! YOU TRY AS LONG AS YOU CAN, BUT THEN YOU MOVE ON!

GOODBYE, "TILL DEATH DO US PART"... ...HELLO, "TILL COUPLES THERAPY MONEY RUNNETH OUT".

I REALLY TRIED TO HEAR WHAT YOU SAID YESTERDAY, CATHY.
YOU DID, ALEX?

YOU'RE NERVOUS ABOUT AGREEING TO MARRY A MAN SO MUCH YOUNGER THAN YOU, AND MY FLIPPANT ATTITUDE TOWARD THE INSTITUTION ONLY VALIDATED WHAT YOU PERCEIVE TO BE AN IRRECONCILABLE GAP IN OUR SENSIBILITIES.
YOU UNDERSTOOD THAT??

OF COURSE! IN AN INCREASINGLY DISPOSABLE AND UNSURE WORLD, YOU LONG FOR SECURITY AND STABILITY. YOU NEED A TANGIBLE, LASTING, PERMANENT COMMITMENT.
OH, ALEX, YOU'RE...

SO I HAD YOUR NAME TATTOOED ON MY BICEP!
THE CURSE OF YOUTH... ALL THE LANGUAGE SKILLS, NONE OF THE JUDGMENT FUNCTIONS.

COOKIES!
NO COOKIES. WE'RE BUYING A NICE, NUTRITIOUS DINNER TONIGHT.
COOKIES!
COOKIES!
COOKIES!
I RESPECT YOUR RIGHT TO VERBALIZE FOOD PREFERENCES, BUT I SAID NO COOKIES!
COOKIES!
COOKIES!
COOKIES!
COOKIES!
COOKIES!
COOKIES!
I WILL BUY THE COOKIES, BUT THE BOX STAYS SEALED UNTIL AFTER DINNER, AND THEN ONE AND ONLY ONE COOKIE!!!
SELF-PARENTING TAKES AN UGLY TURN IN THE SNACK AISLE.
COOKIES!
Guisewite

WHITE ROSES! MONOGRAMMED DOILIES! LACE RICE POUCHES! RUFFLED GARTER! HEART-SHAPED HORS D'OEUVRES!!

UNDER THE VEIL OF QUIET SANITY LURKS THE SOUL OF A BABBLING BRIDE.
Guisewite

A RING!! HE GAVE YOU AN ENGAGEMENT RING!!!
I DIDN'T SAY YES, CHARLENE. HOW COULD I??

A RING! SHE GOT A RING!
I'M SO UNSURE. IT JUST DOESN'T SEEM RIGHT.

IT'S A RING! A RING! A RING!
I'M WRACKED WITH DOUBT! TORMENTED! ANGUISHED! PLEASE! I NEED SOMEONE TO TALK TO!!
RECEPTION

LET ME TRY ON THE RING!!
EVERYONE WANTS A PIECE OF THE ROCK, BUT NO ONE WANTS A CHUNK OF THE PUDDLE.
RECEPTION
Guisewite

I THOUGHT YOU LOVED ALEX, CATHY.
I LOVED HIM UNTIL THE SECOND HE PROPOSED, CHARLENE.

THEN, SUDDENLY, REALITY WAS STANDING RIGHT IN FRONT OF ME. ANXIETY SHOWED UP. FEAR STARTED CALLING.

PANIC POUNDED ON MY FRONT DOOR... AND WHEN I PEEKED OUTSIDE, PARANOIA WRAPPED ITS ARMS AROUND ME AND BEGGED ME TO GO AWAY FOR THE WEEKEND!

AS SOON AS ONE MAN IS READY TO COMMIT, ALL THE OTHER SUITORS COME OUT OF THE WOODWORK.
AT LEAST I KNOW I'M WANTED.
Guisewite

...WELL, YOU COULD TRY BEING ENGAGED AND SEE IF YOU WARM UP TO HIM, SWEETIE!
I LIKE HIM, MOM. WE JUST HAVE NOTHING IN COMMON.

...WELL, YOU COULD TRY BEING ENGAGED AND SEE IF YOU CAN DEVELOP SOME HOBBIES TOGETHER!
MOM, HE WORKS PART TIME AT A GYM AND LIVES WITH HIS MOTHER.

WELL, YOU COULD JUST TRY BEING ENGAGED!! THE RING IS RIGHT HERE! LOOK HOW SPARKLY IT IS!! JUST TRY! TRY FOR YOUR MAMA!!

WHICH IS WORSE, A WOMAN BLINDED BY LOVE, OR A MOTHER BLINDED BY CUBIC ZIRCONIA...
Guisewite

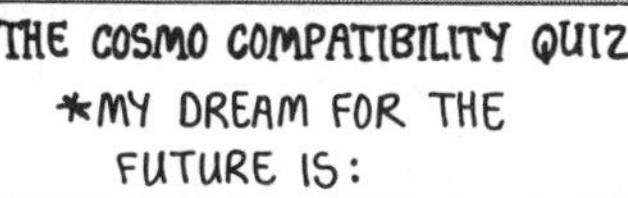
THE COSMO COMPATIBILITY QUIZ
*MY DREAM FOR THE FUTURE IS:

TWO CHILDREN, A BIG, COZY HOUSE, FINANCIAL SECURITY!
A BACKPACK TRIP ACROSS SPAIN!

*MY PERFECT EVENING IS:

A QUIET DINNER AT A ROMANTIC RESTAURANT!
A KICK-BOX CLASS TO RAP MUSIC!
COSMOPOLITAN

*I BELIEVE MARRIAGE IS:

A DEEP, ETERNAL, LIFETIME COMMITMENT!
A REALLY COOL PARTY AND THEN, WHO KNOWS??

THE COSMO GUIDE TO MAKING LOVE LAST:
*NEVER TAKE A COMPATIBILITY QUIZ TOGETHER.
Guisewite

...WAIT!! I DIDN'T BREAK UP, ALEX! I JUST SAID I'M NOT READY TO GET MARRIED!
WELL, WE CAN'T GO BACK TO NORMAL, CATHY.

WHY NOT?? TEN BILLION WOMEN HAVE ASKED FOR A COMMITMENT, BEEN TURNED DOWN, AND BEEN WILLING TO GO BACK TO NORMAL!

THAT'S HOW IT WORKS! YOU SLIDE BACK INTO THE SAME RUTS... DO THE SAME THINGS... AND THEN WAIT FOR THE EXACT SAME PERSON TO FEEL COMPLETELY DIFFERENT AT SOME VAGUE POINT IN THE FUTURE!

THAT'S RIDICULOUS.

INCREDIBLE... EVEN THOUGH THEY CREATED IT, MEN ARE DETERMINED TO REBEL AGAINST THE SYSTEM.

Guisewite

WHERE IS IT?? WHERE'S OUR RING??
I GAVE IT BACK.

GAVE IT BACK?? YOU GAVE BACK OUR ENGAGEMENT RING??
YOU KNOW IT WASN'T RIGHT, MOM.

I THOUGHT I'D AT LEAST GET TO SEE IT AGAIN!! IT CAN'T BE GONE!!
IT'S GONE, MOM.

CHILDREN NEVER HOLD THE POSE LONG ENOUGH FOR THE CHRISTMAS CARD PHOTO.

YOU COULDN'T TRY BEING ENGAGED TO ALEX, CATHY??
YOU INSTILLED ME WITH HIGH STANDARDS, MOM.

YOU COULDN'T OVERLOOK A FEW LITTLE FLAWS??
YOU TAUGHT ME THAT I DESERVED THE BEST.

YOU COULDN'T JUST GIVE IT A WHIRL??
YOU GAVE ME THE VALUES, DISCRETION, SELF-RESPECT AND PATIENCE TO WAIT UNTIL THE END OF TIME FOR A MAN WHO'S WORTHY OF MY HEART!

NEVER THE MOTHER OF THE BRIDE... ...ALWAYS THE MENTOR OF THE BRIDE.

TIME SPENT "GIVING JEFF HIS SPACE"... 2 YEARS, 11 MONTHS.
TAP TAP

TIME SPENT "SEEING WHERE IT GOES WITH IRVING"... 5 YEARS, 7½ MONTHS.
TAP TAP

TIME SPENT "GETTING TO KNOW ALEX"... 1 YEAR, 1¼ MONTH.
TAP TAP

OUT OF A UNIVERSE OF 15 MILLION POTENTIAL MATES, 3 CANDIDATES HAVE USED UP 9.7 YEARS!

SOONER OR LATER, WE ALL REGRET GIVING MOM THE CALCULATOR COIN PURSE.
GOOD NEWS, DEAR! AT THE CURRENT RATE, WE'LL HAVE A WEDDING BY THE YEAR 3792!

UH, OH. IT LOOKS LIKE THE BREAKUP WAS TOUGH, CATHY.
RECEPTI

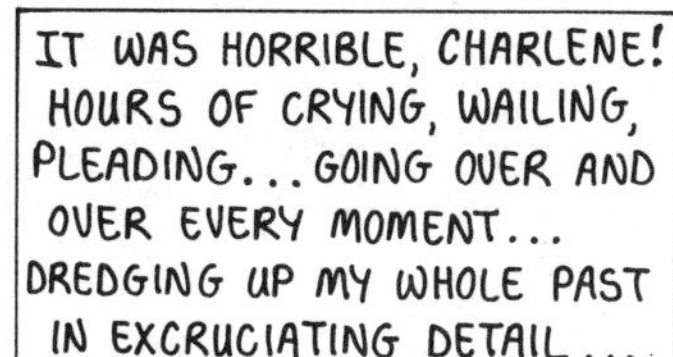
IT WAS HORRIBLE, CHARLENE! HOURS OF CRYING, WAILING, PLEADING... GOING OVER AND OVER EVERY MOMENT... DREDGING UP MY WHOLE PAST IN EXCRUCIATING DETAIL...

IT'S ALWAYS HARDEST ON THE MOTHERS.
YOU'RE TOO OLD TO START OVER, SWEETIE!!
WE'LL TALK ABOUT IT AGAIN TONIGHT, MOM! I PROMISE!
RECEPTION
Guisewite

JUST BECAUSE YOU REJECTED ALEX'S PROPOSAL AND HE DUMPED YOU DOESN'T MEAN IT'S OVER, CATHY...
Diet

...YOUR EYES COULD MEET ACROSS A CROWDED ROOM AND IGNITE A PASSION YOU'VE NEVER KNOWN... YOU COULD RUN INTO EACH OTHER ON A RAINY, DESOLATE HIGHWAY AND BE DRENCHED IN A THUNDER-STORM OF LOVE...

I HAVE A CLIPPING IN MY PURSE ABOUT A COUPLE WHO BROKE UP IN THEIR TEENS AND THEN REUNITED AND GOT MARRIED WHEN THEY WERE 82 YEARS OLD!!
Diet

SOME PEOPLE READ ROMANCE NOVELS. I JUST FLIP OPEN MY MOTHER.
Diet
Guisewite

I'M WORRIED ABOUT CATHY, DEAR.

WHY? IS SHE UPSET?
NO.
IS SHE DEPRESSED?
NO.
DOES SHE HAVE MONEY PROBLEMS?
NO.
HEALTH PROBLEMS?
NO.
WORK PROBLEMS?
NO.

ANY PROBLEMS OF ANY KIND THAT SHE SEEMS UNABLE OR UNWILLING TO HANDLE?
NO.

WHEW! IT'S A WONDER YOU CAN SLEEP AT NIGHT!
FOR SOME, WORRY IS A BIRTHRIGHT. FOR A MOTHER, IT'S AN I-GAVE-BIRTH-RIGHT.
Guisewite

DID YOU THINK ANY-MORE ABOUT US, CATHY ?
ARE YOU KID-DING, ALEX ? IT'S ALL I'VE THOUGHT ABOUT.

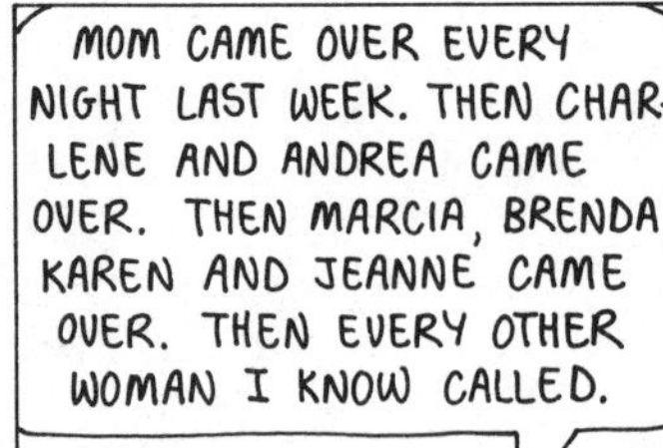
MOM CAME OVER EVERY NIGHT LAST WEEK. THEN CHAR-LENE AND ANDREA CAME OVER. THEN MARCIA, BRENDA, KAREN AND JEANNE CAME OVER. THEN EVERY OTHER WOMAN I KNOW CALLED.

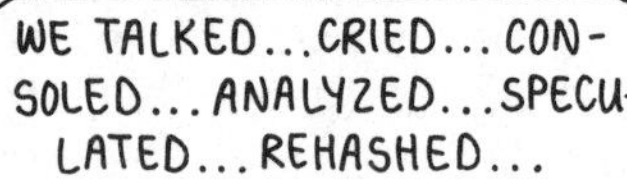
WE TALKED... CRIED... CON-SOLED... ANALYZED... SPECU-LATED... REHASHED...

I THOUGHT YOU NEEDED TIME TO YOURSELF.
MEN GO INTO THEIR CAVE ALONE. WOMEN GO INTO THEIR CAVE WITH 15 GIRLFRIENDS.

I'M SO SORRY I HURT YOU, ALEX. I JUST WASN'T READY TO MARRY YOU.
I WASN'T HURT, CATHY.

IT MUST HAVE BEEN SO HARD FOR YOU. I'M SO VERY, VERY SORRY!
IT WASN'T HARD. I'M FINE.

PLEASE OPEN UP TO ME, ALEX! TELL ME HOW I BROKE YOUR HEART! MAKE ME SUFFER! PLEASE! I WANT TO SUFFER!!
IT JUST DIDN'T WORK OUT. I'M COOL WITH THAT!

AACK! REJECTED! MY GUILT HAS BEEN REJECTED!!
THERE, THERE. YOU'RE A VERY SPECIAL WOMAN. YOU'LL HAVE LOTS OF OTH-ER CHANCES.

YOU'RE PICK-ING UP YOUR STUFF AND WALKING OUT JUST LIKE THAT, ALEX??
IF YOU CAN'T COMMIT TO ME NOW, YOU NEVER WILL.

WHY RUSH OFF?? LET'S SIT AND TALK!
WHAT'S THERE TO TALK ABOUT? THE RELATIONSHIP IS OVER.

WELL, LET'S JUST SIT FOR A MIN-UTE. YOU KNOW... ...REFLECT! ABSORB THE MOMENT!
NAH... I HAVE TO GET GOING.

MEN TAKE OFF AT THE END OF THE PICTURE. WOMEN LIKE TO SIT THROUGH THE FINAL CREDITS.

200 SYMPHONIES...
1500 ART MUSEUMS...
700 PLAYS...
33 OPERAS...
4 YEARS OF COLLEGE...
150 SEMINARS...
20 WORKSHOPS...
5000 BOOKS...
diet
A LIFETIME OF STUDYING, READING, PUSHING, REACHING AND GROWING, AND I HAVE FINALLY BECOME ONE WITH MY TRUE POTENTIAL...
...HUMAN REFRIGERATOR MAGNET.
Guisewite

WHEN THE PASSION FADES, THE THRILL WANES, THE LUST DIMS, THE GIDDINESS DWINDLES...

...YOU ARE READY TO EXPERIENCE THE RICHER, DEEPER, MOST MEANINGFUL PHASE OF LOVE...

THE ETERNAL FLAME OF TOTAL BEWILDERMENT.

DOES THIS LOOK BETTER OR DOES THIS LOOK BETTER?

IS THIS BETTER, OR IS THIS BETTER? OR IS THIS BETTER?

THIS ONE? OR THIS ONE? OR THIS ONE? OR THIS ONE?

THE 7:00AM EYE EXAM
BRING ME MY SUN-GLASSES! THE WHOLE ROOM IS BLURRY!

SPRING IS IN THE AIR, AND I AM READY FOR RENEWAL!

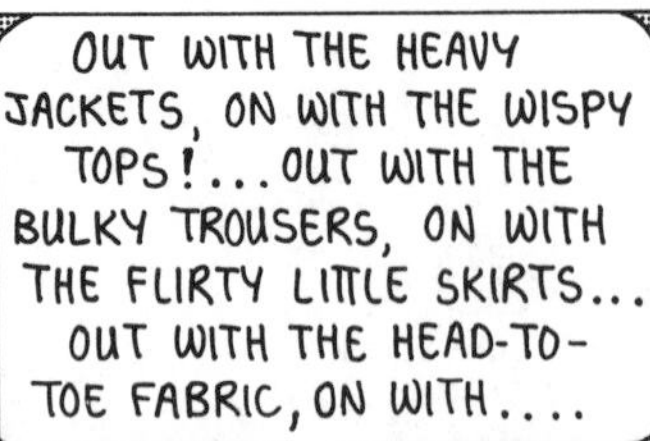
OUT WITH THE HEAVY JACKETS, ON WITH THE WISPY TOPS!... OUT WITH THE BULKY TROUSERS, ON WITH THE FLIRTY LITTLE SKIRTS... OUT WITH THE HEAD-TO-TOE FABRIC, ON WITH....

AACK!

CATHY WILL BE A BIT LATE. SHE JUST GOT HER SPRING BODY OUT OF STORAGE.
RECEPTIONIST

I DREAMED OF A WARDROBE THAT WOULD GRACEFULLY TAKE ME FROM WINTER TO SPRING... I GOT THREE TWEED SPORTCOATS AND SEVEN STRIPED TANK TOPS.

I DREAMED OF A TIDY LINEUP OF BREEZY SKIRTS AND MATCHING SWEATERS...
...I GOT ONE GAUZE SKIRT THAT GOES WITH NOTHING, AND A PILE OF SWEATSHIRTS.

I DREAMED OF A WALK-IN CLOSET. I GOT A SIT-IN CLOSET.
Guisewite

I NEED SOME NEW CLOTHES, CHARLENE.
NO YOU DON'T. YOU NEED A NEW MAN.
RECEPTI

IT'S CLASSIC. WHEN A WOMAN FEELS AN EMOTIONAL VOID, SHE GOES LOOKING FOR SOME NEW OUTFIT TO FILL IT.

I WILL NOT STAND BY AND WATCH YOU THROW MONEY AWAY ON CLOTHES INSTEAD OF FACING YOUR RECENT RELATIONSHIP BLUNDER AND THE NEED TO OPEN YOUR HEART TO SOMEONE ELSE!!

YOU'RE RIGHT. I NEED A NEW MAN.
GOOD. NOW YOU NEED SOME NEW CLOTHES.
RECEPTION
Guisewite

WELCOME TO SPRING '95! HARKEN BACK TO THE DAYS OF ELEGANCE AND GLAMOUR!
SPRING

HARKEN BACK TO THE DAYS OF SOPHISTICATION AND HEAD-TO-TOE FEMININITY!
SPRING

HARKEN BACK TO THE DAYS WHEN PEOPLE HAD SOME MONEY, SOME TIME, AND SOMEPLACE TO WEAR A GETUP LIKE THAT!
Guisewite

HARKEN BACK TO THE DAYS WHEN CUSTOMERS KEPT THEIR LITTLE MOUTHS SHUT.
SPRIN

ALL YOU NEED TO KNOW ABOUT SPRING FASHION IS THAT SHOULDER PADS ARE NOW WORN ON THE CHEST.
IN
OUT

A WOMAN'S POWER SOURCE HAS SHIFTED, LITERALLY, FROM BEEFY SHOULDERS TO A BOOMING BUST.
IN

IF MEN IN THE WORKPLACE WEREN'T INTIMIDATED BY OUR POWER SUITS, HA, HA !! WAIT TILL THEY GET A LOAD OF THE POWER BOSOM !!

WHAT ABOUT THE LAST TWO DECADES OF FIGHTING FOR RESPECT?
NOT A PROBLEM. THE CORSET WAIST CUTS OFF ALL CIRCULATION TO THE BRAIN.
IN
OUT

THE SKINNY BELT! THIS SEASON'S MUST-HAVE ACCESSORY!
MUST HAVE?

YES! SEE? TO WEAR IT, YOU MUST HAVE A WAISTLINE... MUST HAVE A FLAT STOMACH... MUST HAVE A TONED REAR END...

...AND YOU MUST HAVE NO FLAB WHATSOEVER BETWEEN YOUR NECK AND KNEES!

IT ALWAYS RUINS FASHION TO HAVE IT EXPLAINED.
THE NEW BELT

POWERFUL SENSUALITY! PROVOCATIVE GLAMOUR! OUTRAGEOUS ELEGANCE! SPRING FASHION CAPTURES THE HEART AND SOUL OF THE AMERICAN WOMAN!
SPRING '95

I SEE... HOWEVER, KNOWING THAT 80% OF AMERICAN WOMEN THINK WE'RE OVERWEIGHT, AND 99% OF THE 80% ARE MOST SENSITIVE ABOUT OUR HIPS, WHY WOULD EVERY SINGLE TOP FOR SPRING END JUST ABOVE THE WIDEST PART OF THE REAR?

WE CAPTURE THE HEART AND SOUL! THE FLESH IS YOUR PROBLEM!!
Elegant

AFTER THE DREARY PRISON OF DUMPY, FRUMPY, DEPRESSING GRUNGE, WOMEN ARE FINALLY FREE TO BE WOMEN AGAIN!

FREE TO DRESS UP IN CHIC LITTLE JACKETS! FREE TO SLITHER INTO FIGURE HUGGING SKIRTS! FREE TO FLAUNT EVERY CURVE!

I CAN'T BREATHE, BEND, SIT, OR WALK.
PERFECT! WHEEL HER OUT ONTO THE SIDEWALK AND LET THE FLIRTATION BEGIN!!
Guisewite

NOTHING MIRRORS OUR EMANCIPATION FROM THE WORKAHOLIC '80s AND OUR QUEST FOR THE '90s QUALITY OF LIFE LIKE THE REDEFINED WOMAN'S SUIT!
NEW

EVERY FEMININE INCH SAYS, "OH, SURE, I MAY BE GOING TO A BOARD MEETING, BUT I MAY ALSO BE POPPING OUT FOR TEA... I MAY GO STROLL THE MUSEUM... I MAY SPEND THE AFTERNOON AT THE THEATRE..."

IN SHORT, IT'S BUSINESS ATTIRE THAT SAYS, "I HAVE BETTER THINGS TO DO WITH MY LIFE THAN SIT IN THIS BORING OFFICE!"

FOR INSTANCE, I COULD GO STAND IN THE UNEMPLOYMENT LINE.
OH, HA, HA! HERE. HOT PINK! YOUR LIPS STILL LOOK A BIT SERIOUS!
Guisewite

IT'S TOO DONE-UP FOR THE OFFICE... TOO DRESSY FOR A DATE... AND TOO IMPRACTICAL FOR EVERYTHING ELSE.

AH, BUT HOW PERFECT TO WEAR WHILE STANDING ON THE PLATFORM WAITING FOR THE TRAIN THAT WILL TAKE YOU, YOUR BOUQUET OF HYDRANGEAS AND YOUR MATCHING FOUR-PIECE LUGGAGE SET TO A REUNION WITH YOUR LONG-LOST LOVE IN THE SOUTH OF FRANCE!

YES! PERFECT! IT WOULD BE PERFECT!
MEN BUY CLOTHES. WOMEN BUY SCENARIOS.
Guisewite

MY COMPANY'S FINALLY RELAXED ENOUGH, AND I'M SECURE ENOUGH TO WEAR PANTS EVERY DAY TO THE OFFICE!
PANTS ARE HISTORY.

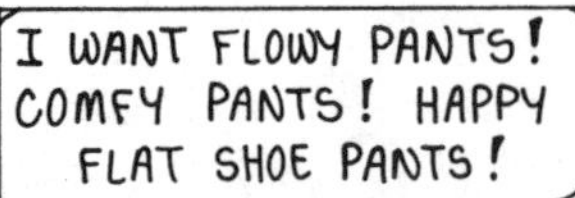
I WANT FLOWY PANTS! COMFY PANTS! HAPPY FLAT SHOE PANTS!

FLOWY'S HISTORY. COMFY'S HISTORY. FLATS ARE HISTORY.

THIS SPRING'S LOOK IS THE SLINKY, MID-KNEE SKIRT OF THE 1940'S! SEE?? IT'S HISTORY! YOU CAN WEAR A PIECE OF HISTORY!

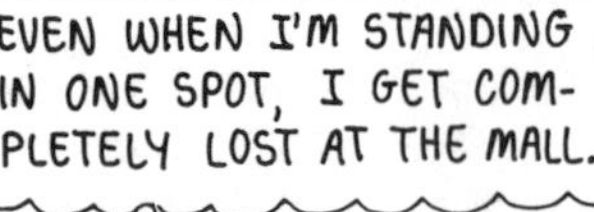
EVEN WHEN I'M STANDING IN ONE SPOT, I GET COMPLETELY LOST AT THE MALL.

THE NEW RETRO

THANKS, BUT I'M GOING TO LOOK AROUND A LITTLE.

LOOK AROUND AS IN, YOU DON'T SEE ANYTHING YOU LIKE AND WANT TO LOOK AROUND?...OR, LOOK AROUND AS IN, YOU SEE SOMETHING YOU LIKE AND WANT TO FIND IT CHEAPER SOMEWHERE ELSE?...

...OR LOOK AROUND AS IN, AFTER USING UP TWO HOURS OF MY TIME AND EVERY SPECK OF MY PATIENCE BECOMING EDUCATED ON THE "LOOK," YOU WANT TO BREEZE INTO SOMEONE ELSE'S DEPARTMENT AND PLUCK AN OUTFIT OFF THE RACK??

ALL OF THE ABOVE.
THEY ONLY GO FOR THE TOTAL CONCEPT WHEN IT'S TO ANNOY THE SALES CLERK.

TOO EAGER.

TOO ALOOF.

TOO INSINCERE.

TOO INTIMIDATING.

AS THE DOORS OPEN ON ANOTHER THRILLING WEEK IN THE WORLD OF WOMEN'S WEAR, THE SALES FORCE PREPARES TO PRESENT THE SPRING LOOK.
MAY I HELP YOU?
SPRING

TOO CALCULATED.
TOO PICKY!
TOO GROUCHY.
SPRING

IF SHE'S JUST HAVING PASTA, THEN I'LL JUST HAVE THE CHOPPED SALAD.
MENU
MENU

IF SHE'S JUST HAVING A CHOPPED SALAD, THEN CHANGE MINE TO A CHOPPED SALAD WITH NO **MEAT**!
MAKE MINE WITH NO MEAT AND NO **CHEESE**!
MENU
Guisewite

NO MEAT, NO CHEESE, NO CROUTONS, NO DRESSING!! JUST **LETTUCE**!
MAKE MINE A **TINY** BOWL OF LETTUCE!
MENU
MENU

HEALTHY COMPETITION: GOOD FOR PEOPLE, BAD FOR BUSINESS.
NO FOOD! JUST ICED TEA!
NO TEA! JUST WATER!

DID YOU EVER SEE A PICTURE OF YOUR GRANDMA FLOPPING AROUND IN A SWEATSUIT?... ...NO. DID YOUR MOTHER'S YEARBOOK SHOW HER HANGING OUT IN FLIP-FLOPS AND A BASEBALL CAP?...NO.
The New Glamour

THE PROUD, BEAUTIFUL WOMEN OF OUR PAST HAD AN ELEGANCE OF SPIRIT THAT'S CAPTURED IN EVERY BIT OF SPRING FASHION!

IT ISN'T DRESSING FOR MEN. IT ISN'T DRESSING FOR WOMEN. IT'S DRESSING FOR THE ONE THING THAT REALLY MATTERS...
4

DO IT FOR THE PHOTO ALBUM!
IN WHICH CASE YOU'LL ALSO WANT TO BE STOPPING BY THE COSMETICS COUNTER.

YES! DARING ELEGANCE! FLIRTATIOUS GLAMOUR!
THIS IS MY SLIP.

YES! OWN IT! MAKE IT YOUR OWN!
I DO OWN IT! THIS IS MY SLIP!

TOSS ON A SHRUNKEN SWEATER... KICK ON SOME HEELS, AND STRUT YOUR STUFF INTO SPRING!
I BOUGHT THIS SLIP FIVE YEARS AGO! THIS ISN'T A SLIP DRESS! THIS IS MY SLIP!

YOU ALREADY OWN IT?? AACK! IN THAT CASE, IT'S INDECENT!
GOOD TO KNOW RETAIL STILL KNOWS WHERE TO DRAW THE LINE.
Guisewite

MEN LIVE LIFE DIFFERENTLY BECAUSE THEY'RE TALLER. IT'S AS SIMPLE AS THAT.

BUT WITH THE NEW HIGHER HEEL, WOMEN CAN EXPERIENCE THE SAME KIND OF POWER. SEE?? YOU CAN BE TALL! YOU CAN BE AUTHORITATIVE! YOU CAN BE COMMANDING!
SHOES

BRING ME A CELLULAR PHONE AND THE NUMBER OF A PODIATRIST! MY TOES HAVE BEEN CRUSHED INTO LITTLE POINTS!!
...AND YET, STILL RETAIN AN AIR OF VULNERABILITY!
SHOES
Guisewite

NO, I AM NOT INTERESTED IN "THIS SPRING'S ESSENTIAL TEENY-WEENY HANDBAG."

IT NOT ONLY DEMEANS THE COMPLEXITY OF LIFE BY IMPLYING IT'S JUST AN ORGANIZATION PROBLEM... BUT INSULTS US INDIVIDUALLY BY PRESUMING THAT ANY WOMAN COULD BREEZE THROUGH 1995 WITH NOTHING MORE THAN LIPSTICK AND A HANKIE.

WOMEN COPE WITH ENOUGH WITHOUT HAVING TO SMASH IT ALL INTO A FOUR-INCH HANDBAG!!
LOOK! IT PERFECTLY MATCHES THE SHOES!

IT MATCHES THE SHOES??
THE SEARCH FOR JUSTICE IS NOTHING COMPARED TO THE QUEST FOR COORDINATES.

"BEAUTY IS AN ATTITUDE, NOT AN OUTFIT," WE TOLD THEM.

"DEVELOP YOUR OWN INDIVIDUAL STYLE!" WE CHEERED... "ANYTHING GOES! WEAR ANYTHING AT ALL!!"
NEW

WE MADE THE AMERICAN WOMAN FEEL SO GOOD ABOUT HERSELF SHE NOT ONLY QUIT DEPENDING ON OUR SUPPORT AND APPROVAL, SHE DOESN'T EVEN COME VISIT ANYMORE!
NEW

1995: RETAIL GOES FROM RECESSION TO EMPTY NEST SYNDROME.
NEW

HELLO, CLOTHES. THIS IS MY NEW ULTRA-GLAMOROUS, PROVOCATIVELY FEMININE, PROFOUNDLY CHIC SUIT.

EVEN THOUGH MANY OF YOU HAVE WAITED FOR YEARS FOR SOME ATTENTION FROM ME, I'M SURE YOU'LL UNDERSTAND IF I SHOVE YOU ALL ASIDE SO I CAN HANG MY NEW SUIT IN ITS OWN, PRISTINE SPACE.

SNAP.

LIFE IS ALWAYS TOUGH ON THE NEWCOMER.

COME ON IN, MOM. I WAS JUST CLEANING MY CLOSET.
I HAVE THE SPRING CLEANING BUG MYSELF, CATHY.

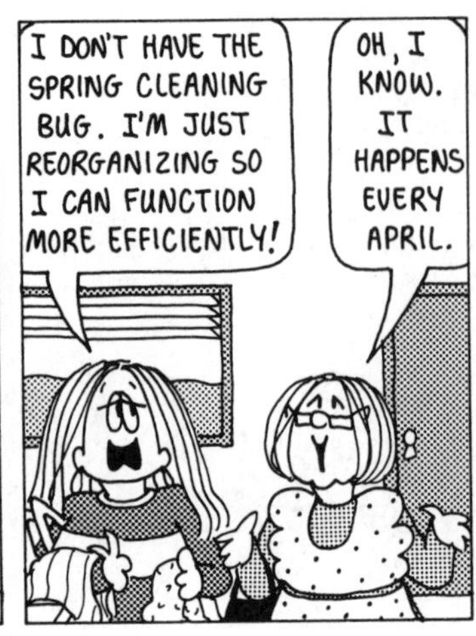
I DON'T HAVE THE SPRING CLEANING BUG. I'M JUST REORGANIZING SO I CAN FUNCTION MORE EFFICIENTLY!
OH, I KNOW. IT HAPPENS EVERY APRIL.

MOTHER, I MIGHT BE DOING THE EXACT SAME THING YOU'RE DOING, BUT I'M DOING IT FOR A DIFFERENT REASON AND IT IS PURELY COINCIDENCE THAT I'M DOING IT AT THE SAME TIME!!

THE CLASSIC WARBLING OF SPRING: MOTHER NATURE VERSUS DAUGHTER DEFIANCE.

TA, DA! MY NEW SUIT!
BRING IT CLOSER. I PROMISE I WON'T LOOK AT THE PRICE TAG.

YOU CAN SEE THE SUIT FROM HERE, MOM.
OH, FOR HEAVEN'S SAKE, CATHY. I'M NOT GOING TO LOOK AT THE PRICE TAG.

IT'S NONE OF MY BUSINESS HOW YOU SPEND YOUR MONEY. I JUST WANT TO SEE THE...

AACK!! $500!!
IT'S NONE OF HER BUSINESS, HOWEVER, IT'S A RELATED INDUSTRY...

HOW COULD YOU BUY THIS EXPENSIVE NEW SUIT WHEN YOU HAVE ALL THESE PERFECTLY NICE CLOTHES, CATHY??
THOSE ARE ALL GOING OUT, MOM.

OUT?? THIS JACKET'S HARDLY BEEN WORN! THIS DRESS IS AS GOOD AS NEW! WITH A FEW ALTERATIONS, THESE PANTS COULD BE WORN FOR YEARS!

I SAY WE MARCH RIGHT BACK TO THE STORE AND UNLOAD THE MISTAKE WHILE YOU STILL CAN!!

HELLO. I'D LIKE TO RETURN MY MOTHER.
Women's

YOU WOULDN'T BELIEVE WHAT IT'S LIKE TRYING TO HELP CATHY CLEAN HER CLOSET.

SHE REJECTS MY OPINION, DISAGREES WITH MY IDEAS, REBELS AGAINST MY ADVICE, AND RIDICULES MY SYSTEM...

...AND YET, BY THE END, IT ALL BALANCED OUT IN A BEAUTIFUL KIND OF SYMMETRY.

THE LESS OF ME THERE IS IN HER BRAIN, THE MORE OF HER THERE IS IN MY BASEMENT.
SAVE FOR CATHY
CATHY'S
CATHY'S STUFF
SAVE FOR CATHY
CATHY'S STUFF
SAVE FOR CATHY
CATHY'S STUFF
Guisewite

LOOKED FOR SWEATPANTS: 5 MINUTES.
LOOKED FOR SWEATSHIRT: 11 MINUTES.
LOOKED FOR CLEAN SOCKS: 4 MINUTES.
LOOKED FOR TENNIS SHOES: 6 MINUTES.

LOOKED FOR CONTACT CASE: 4 MINUTES.
LOOKED FOR GLASSES: 23 MINUTES.
LOOKED FOR TOOTHPASTE: 7 MINUTES.

LOOKED FOR DELIVERY MENU: 9 MINUTES.
LOOKED FOR CORDLESS PHONE: 13 MINUTES.
LOOKED FOR CASH: 17 MINUTES.
LOOKED FOR TV GUIDE: 6 MINUTES.
LOOKED FOR REMOTE CONTROL: 8 MINUTES.

ANOTHER FREE EVENING SACRIFICED TO THE GOD OF DISORGANIZATION.

I'M SICK OF GOVERNMENT WASTE AND WILL BE PROTESTING BY NOT FILING A TAX RETURN THIS YEAR!

FINE. JUST KNOW THAT IF IT TURNS OUT THE GOVERNMENT OWES YOU MONEY AND YOU DON'T FILE YOUR CLAIM, ITS DEBT TO YOU WILL BE CANCELED IN THREE YEARS...

...BUT IF IT TURNS OUT YOU OWE THE GOVERNMENT MONEY AND YOU DON'T PAY UP, YOUR DEBT WILL COMPOUND HOURLY WITH INTEREST AND PENALTIES AND HAUNT YOU UNTIL THE DAY YOU DIE, DRAGGING YOU AND EVERYTHING YOU HOLD DEAR DOWN WITH IT.

I'M HERE TO DO MY TAXES.
THE PROTEST IS OVER. THE DEMONSTRATION IS ABOUT TO BEGIN.
C.P.A.
MISC. RECEIPTS
RECEPTION
Guisewite

I HAVE NOTHING! ZERO! ZILCH! ZIPPO! THE MONEY'S GONE! ALL GONE!
ACCOUNTANT

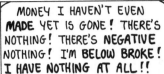

MONEY I HAVEN'T EVEN MADE YET IS GONE! THERE'S NOTHING! THERE'S NEGATIVE NOTHING! I'M BELOW BROKE! I HAVE NOTHING AT ALL!!

I FLING MYSELF ON YOUR MERCY, BELOVED ACCOUNTANT, FOR YOU AND ONLY YOU HOLD MY FUTURE IN YOUR HANDS!!
ACCOUNTANT

PLEASE PAY IN ADVANCE
ACCOUNTANT
Guisewite

FILING STATUS: MARRIED OR SINGLE?
WHAT ABOUT DIVORCED?
TUMS
1994-1040
ACCOUNTANT

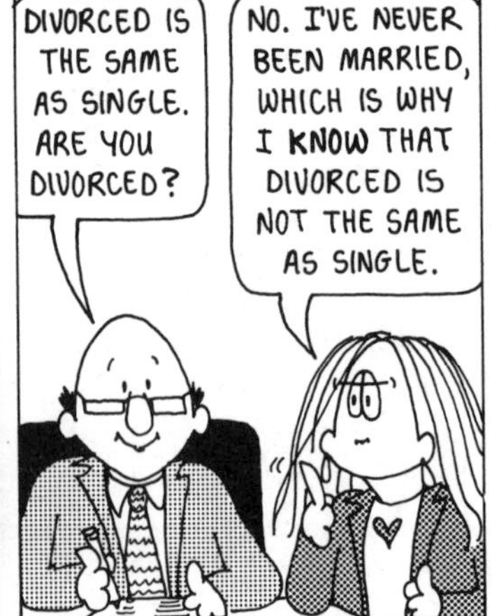
DIVORCED IS THE SAME AS SINGLE. ARE YOU DIVORCED?
NO. I'VE NEVER BEEN MARRIED, WHICH IS WHY I KNOW THAT DIVORCED IS NOT THE SAME AS SINGLE.

DIVORCED PEOPLE AT LEAST HAD SOME WEDDING GIFTS TO SPLIT UP! SINGLE PEOPLE HAVE HAD TO BUY EVERY MISERABLE THING OURSELVES AND SHOULD NOT NOW OR EVER SHARE THE SAME TAX STATUS AS SOMEONE WHO GOT A BRIDAL DRESS AND A FREE BLENDER!!

PERHAPS WE SHOULD START WITH SOMETHING EASIER... ... SAY, THE ENTIRE REST OF THE TAX RETURN?
TUMS
ACCOUNTANT
Guisewite

THE SINGLE MOST RIVETING BIT OF COMPASSION EVER PUBLISHED BY THE I.R.S. IS THIS LITTLE PASSAGE ON THE BACK OF THIS YEAR'S 1040 BOOKLET.
1994-1040
ACCOUNTANT

LOOK AT THIS: IN 1993, THE GOVERNMENT TOOK IN $1,154 BILLION AND SPENT $1,408 BILLION, LEAVING IT $254 BILLION IN THE HOLE.
1994-1040

IT'S THE GOVERNMENT'S WAY OF SAYING, "NO MATTER HOW BADLY YOU'VE BLOWN IT, WE'VE BLOWN IT WORSE! WE UNDERSTAND! WE'VE BEEN THERE! WE'RE RIGHT DOWN THERE IN THE GUTTER WITH YOU!!!"
1994-1040

THEY BLEW IT USING MY MONEY!
GO AHEAD AND CRY. IT HELPS BLUR THE ACCOMPANYING PIE-CHART CONFESSIONAL.
1994-1040
Guisewite

EXCESSIVE DIETING HAS RESULTED IN LOSS OF MUSCLE TISSUE WHICH HAS SLOWED MY METABOLIC RATE AND MADE WEIGHT LOSS VIRTUALLY IMPOSSIBLE!
SALAD BAR
AN OVERPRODUCTION OF INSULIN IS INHIBITING THE LIPOPROTEIN LIPASE AND CAUSING MY BODY TO BURN CARBOHYDRATES INSTEAD OF FAT!
SALAD BAR
A BIOCHEMICAL IMBALANCE OF THE NEUROTRANSMITTER SERTONIN IS CREATING UNCONTROLLABLE CRAVINGS AND APPETITE!
BAR
ANOTHER SESSION OF THE LUNCH-HOUR SCIENTISTS...
ENZYME MALFUNCTION!
GENE MUTATION!
DESSERT MENU!
Guisewite

THIS YEAR, THE AVERAGE TAX-PAYER WILL PAY $1,932.00 EXTRA TO COVER THE $150 BILLION THAT THE CHEATERS AND DEADBEATS DON'T PAY.
I'M FINANCING THE CHEATERS AND DEADBEATS??

OR, IF YOU PREFER, WE COULD EARMARK YOUR $1,932.00 TO HELP FUND THE SLACKERS AND BUMBLERS WHO SPENT $1 BILLION TRYING TO FIND THE CHEATERS AND DEADBEATS.
THE BUMBLERS SPENT $1 BILLION AND DIDN'T FIND THE DEADBEATS??

OR, WE COULD THROW YOUR $1,932.00 IN THE POT AND LET IT BE A KIND OF CHEATER-DEADBEAT-SLACKER-BUMBLER FREE-FOR-ALL!!
OH, WHO CARES? WHAT'S THE DIFFERENCE? LET SOMEONE ELSE DECIDE!
TAX WORKBOOK

SEE? THAT'S THE PROBLEM WITH THIS COUNTRY. NO ONE TAKES RESPONSIBILITY.
ACCOUNTANT

IF I WEREN'T SO DISORGANIZED, I COULD HAVE SAVED SOME MONEY THIS YEAR.
Receipts
ACCOUNTANT

IF I FELT BETTER ABOUT MYSELF, I WOULDN'T BE SO DISORGANIZED.
Receipts
ACCOUNTANT

IF I BOUGHT THOSE CUTE SHOES, I'D FEEL BETTER ABOUT MYSELF. OFF I GO TO THE MALL!!
Receipts
ACCOUNTANT

A WORLD RECORD: 6.3 SECONDS.

WHEN YOU TAKE THE JOURNEY THIS OFTEN, YOU LEARN ALL THE SHORTCUTS.

Receipts

ACCOUNTANT

YOUR INVESTMENT PLAN FOR 1995?

ENTER PUBLISHERS CLEARINGHOUSE SWEEPSTAKES.

YOUR FUTURE FINANCIAL GOAL?
WIN PUBLISHERS CLEARINGHOUSE SWEEPSTAKES.
YOUR LONG-TERM MONEY MANAGEMENT STRATEGY?
MOVE TO NEW LOCATION SO FRIENDS AND RELATIVES WON'T MOOCH OFF SWEEPSTAKES WINNINGS.

HAVE YOU NO GRASP OF REALITY WHATSOEVER? AREN'T YOU INTERESTED IN ONE PIECE OF REAL ADVICE??
OF COURSE I WANT REAL ADVICE.

SHOULD I BE TAKING MY MILLIONS IN ONE LUMP SUM, OR SHOULD I BE MARKING THE BOX FOR YEARLY INSTALLMENTS?
ACCOUNTANT

THIS IS CUTE!
$54 ?! YOU MUST BE KIDDING!

I DIDN'T SAY I WAS **GETTING** IT! I JUST THOUGHT IT WAS CUTE!
I CAN'T BELIEVE YOU'RE EVEN **IN A STORE** AFTER THE PROMISES YOU MADE YESTERDAY!!

I WORK HARD FOR MY MONEY! I'LL SPEND IT ANY WAY I WANT!!
YOU'RE THE MOST IRRESPONSIBLE PERSON I EVER MET!

MONEY RUINS THE RELATIONSHIP EVEN WHEN THERE'S ONLY ONE PERSON IN IT.
I CAN'T BELIEVE I HAVE TO GO HOME WITH YOU.
YOU MAKE ME SICK.
HATS
Mall

"LEAVE CONDITIONER ON FOR THREE MINUTES"... HAH! I'M NOT STANDING HERE FOR THREE MINUTES!

"RINSE WITH PLAQUE REMOVER BEFORE BRUSHING"... ... HAH! MAYBE I FEEL LIKE RINSING AFTER BRUSHING!

PLAQUE WASH

"REPLACE CAP"... HAH! I'M NOT IN THE MOOD TO REPLACE THE CAP! THE CAP STAYS OFF!!

SOME CONQUER THE WORLD. I CONQUER THE TOILETRIES.

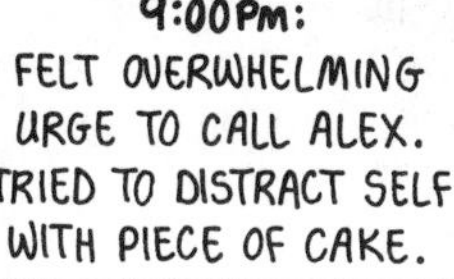
9:00PM:
FELT OVERWHELMING URGE TO CALL ALEX. TRIED TO DISTRACT SELF WITH PIECE OF CAKE.

9:05PM:
CAKE FAILED. TRIED TO REFOCUS BRAIN OFF PHONE AND ONTO BAG OF TOSTITOS.

9:07PM:
TOSTITOS FAILED. TRIED TO SMOTHER URGE UNDER ROLL OF CHOCOLATE CHIP COOKIE DOUGH, BOWL OF POPCORN AND DISH OF ICE CREAM.

9:13PM:
CALLED ALEX. GOT MACHINE. HUNG UP.

I COULD HAVE HUNG ONTO MY WILLPOWER LONGER, BUT I RAN OUT OF FOOD.

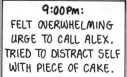

5% RAISE, TWO EXTRA VACATION DAYS AND A KEY TO THE VENDING MACHINE.

DONE.

SECRETARIES' DAY IS LESS THAN 24 HOURS AWAY! GET OUT THERE AND SHOP! RUSH! EMERGENCY!! ASAP! DUE IMMEDIATELY!

DROP EVERYTHING! PRICE IS NO OBJECT! OVERSPEND ON THE PRESENTATION AND PLEDGE TO REFORM TOMORROW!

TOP PRIORITY! NO EXCUSES! NO EXTENSIONS! DEADLINE! DEADLINE!

EVERY OFFICE SPEAKS ITS OWN LANGUAGE. OURS IS PANIC.
Happy Secretaries' Week
Guisewite

I DIDN'T GET YOU ANYTHING FOR SECRETARIES' DAY, CHARLENE, BECAUSE I HAVE TOO MANY CONFLICTING FEELINGS.
GIFTS
Happy Secretaries' Week

ON ONE HAND, YOU DESERVE A SPECIAL TRIBUTE FOR ALL YOUR HARD WORK... BUT ON THE OTHER HAND, YOU EARN LESS THAN ANYONE HERE AND TO BUY YOU OFF WITH SECRETARIES' DAY TRINKETS SEEMS COMPLETELY DEMEANING.

INSTEAD OF A GIFT, I PLEDGE TO TREAT YOU AS AN EQUAL, VALUABLE BUSINESS PEER, AND WORK TOWARD THE DAY WHEN ALL WOMEN IN THE WORKPLACE HAVE THE SALARIES, BENEFITS AND RESPECT WE DESERVE!!

WILL THE FESTIVITIES NEVER END? FIRST CHEAP COLOGNE, NOW ENLIGHTENED GUILT.
GIFTS
Guisewite

HI, MOM. WHAT ARE YOU DOING HERE?
IT'S "TAKE OUR DAUGHTERS TO WORK DAY"! I'VE COME TO TAKE YOU TO YOUR OFFICE!

NO, MOM... THIS IS A DAY TO GIVE GIRLS A LOOK AT WOMEN IN THE WORKPLACE!
AND WHO BETTER TO SHOW YOU OFF THAN YOUR MOTHER??

IT'S FOR DAUGHTERS, MOM! AN INSPIRATIONAL DAY FOR DAUGHTERS!
SHE'S HERE! MY BEAUTIFUL, TALENTED DAUGHTER IS HERE!!

HI. I'M CATHY, AND THIS IS MY MOTHER, A ONE-WOMAN, ONE-CLIENT P.R. FIRM.
WELCOME
Guisewite

ALL I REALLY WANT IS ONE HOUR OF PEACE AND QUIET SO I CAN GET ORGANIZED AND ON TOP OF THINGS FOR ONCE.
IN
Happy Secretaries' Week

JUST ONE BLISSFUL HOUR WITH NO INTERRUPTIONS, NO PHONE CALLS, NO QUESTIONS, NO DELIVERIES, NO PEOPLE STOPPING BY! JUST ONE SOLID HOUR TO MYSELF!

ONE HOUR.
Happy Secretaries' Week

...THAT WAS FOR MY TOP DRAWER. FOR MY 'IN' BASKET AND FILE CABINET, I'LL NEED A SIX-WEEK LEAVE OF ABSENCE.
IN
Happy Secretaries' Week

WHEN I TYPED EVERY DOCUMENT FOR THIS COMPANY, I DID IT ON A $200 MANUAL TYPEWRITER... WHEN YOU GOT INTERESTED IN TYPING NOTES TO PEOPLE, WE GOT A $40,000 COMPUTER SYSTEM...

WHEN I DID ALL THE BOOKKEEPING, IT WAS ME, A PENCIL AND A BOTTLE OF ASPIRIN.. ...WHEN YOU GOT INTERESTED IN TRACKING FINANCES, YOU BOUGHT A $500 MODEM, $600 OF SOFTWARE, AND A $10,000 COLOR PRINTER...

I HANDLED 12 PHONE LINES FOR SIX YEARS... WHEN YOU HAD TO COVER THE PHONES FOR FIVE MINUTES ONE DAY, YOU ORDERED A $7,000 VOICE MAIL SYSTEM.

WHAT'S YOUR POINT, CHARLENE?
GET INTERESTED IN DOING DISHES SO WE CAN GET A DISHWASHER IN THE COFFEE ROOM!!
Happy Secretaries Week

AACK!! THERE'S A GRAY HAIR STICKING STRAIGHT OUT OF MY HEAD!!

...AND A BLEMISH!! I DIDN'T SEE THAT BLEMISH IN THE MIRROR AT HOME!!

...AND WRINKLES!! HOW LONG HAVE I BEEN WALKING AROUND WITH ALL THESE WRINKLES??

A WOMAN, HER FACE, AND FULL SUNLIGHT HAVE AN IN-CAR COLLISION IN THE REARVIEW MIRROR.
EVERY DAY IT'S MORE DANGEROUS TO BE ON THE ROAD.

I HAD TO BORROW 9 GRAMS OF FAT FROM TUESDAY'S ALLOTMENT FOR MONDAY'S BUSINESS DINNER...
diet
1998 FOOD DIAR
FAT GRAMS
I BORROWED 12 GRAMS OF FAT FROM **WEDNESDAY'S** ALLOTMENT FOR TUESDAY'S BIRTHDAY LUNCHEON... AND BORROWED 21 GRAMS OF FAT FROM **FRIDAY'S** ALLOTMENT FOR THURSDAY'S CHEESE-AND-CRACKER CLIENT MEETING.
1995 FOOD
TO DATE, I'VE BORROWED 1,347 GRAMS OF FAT, WHICH IS COMPOUNDING HOURLY AT 18% INTEREST IN MY WAIST, THIGHS AND REAR.
1995
FROM THE NECK UP, I WORRY ABOUT CREDIT CARD DEBT. FROM THE NECK DOWN, FAT DEBT.
1995
FAT GRAMS
Guisewite

BRENDA: ORGANIZES HER OUTFITS FOR THE WEEK EACH SUNDAY AND GROUPS THEM BY DAY WITH MATCHING SHOES, JEWELRY AND ACCESSORIES.

TUES
WED
THURS
FRI

SUSAN: LAYS OUT HER CLOTHES THE NIGHT BEFORE, DOING ANY NEEDED PRESSING OR MENDING.

JEANNE: DECIDES WHAT TO WEAR BEFORE POPPING INTO THE SHOWER IN THE MORNING.

CATHY: STILL CHANGING HER MIND AT 3:00 IN THE AFTERNOON.

WOULD HAVE BEEN HAPPIER IN THE BLUE PANTS... NO... SHOULD HAVE GONE WITH THE TAN JACKET... NO... FLATS. SHOULD HAVE WORN FLATS...
Guisewite

I'M HOME, ELECTRA! ARE YOU READY TO GO OUT?? OUTSIDE? GO OUTSIDE??

OUT FOR A WALK?? OUT FOR A RUN?? A BIG RUN?? A BIG RUN IN THE PARK? YES! GET THE LEASH!

...WHEW. JUST A SECOND. I JUST HAVE TO LIE DOWN FOR A SECOND...

THE SHOW NEVER DOES QUITE LIVE UP TO THE PREVIEWS, DOES IT?
Guisewite

MAYBE I WAS WRONG ABOUT ALEX. DO YOU THINK I WAS WRONG ABOUT ALEX?

CATHY, YOU FLIRTED WITH HIM, FOLLOWED HIM, FLUNG YOURSELF AT HIM, WARPED YOUR PERSONALITY TO BE WITH HIM, ABANDONED ALL WOMEN FRIENDS BECAUSE OF HIM, AND THEN WHEN HE PROPOSED, YOU DUMPED HIM!

WERE YOU WRONG ABOUT ALEX?? ISN'T THERE SOME OTHER QUESTION YOU SHOULD BE ASKING AT THIS POINT??
YOU'RE RIGHT.

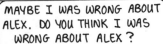

IS GROVELING BENEATH ME OR ABOVE ME?

Guisewite

I COULD CALL ALEX AND ASK HIM OUT TO DINNER. WHY NOT? HA, HA! WHY NOT??

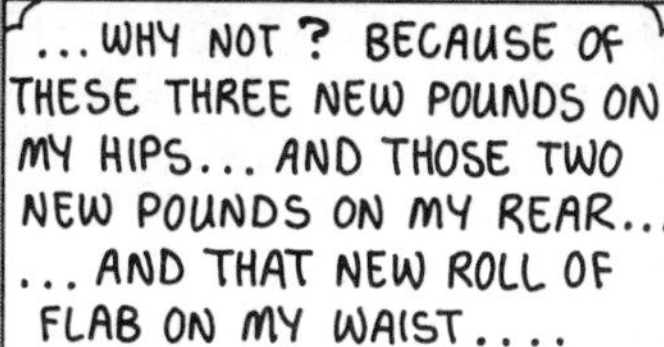
...WHY NOT? BECAUSE OF THESE THREE NEW POUNDS ON MY HIPS... AND THOSE TWO NEW POUNDS ON MY REAR...
...AND THAT NEW ROLL OF FLAB ON MY WAIST....

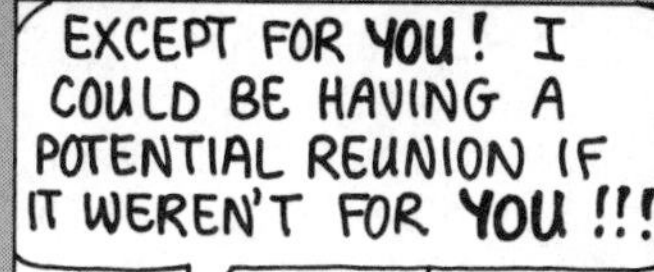
EXCEPT FOR YOU! I COULD BE HAVING A POTENTIAL REUNION IF IT WEREN'T FOR YOU!!!

ANOTHER RELATIONSHIP RUINED BY THE OTHER WOMAN.
Guisewite

DES-SERT?
NO, THANK YOU.
MEMORIAL DAY IS IN A MONTH.

A MONTH IS THE PERFECT WEIGHT-LOSS UNIT!
LONG ENOUGH TO MAKE A VISI-BLE DIFFERENCE, BUT SHORT ENOUGH TO BE BEARABLE!

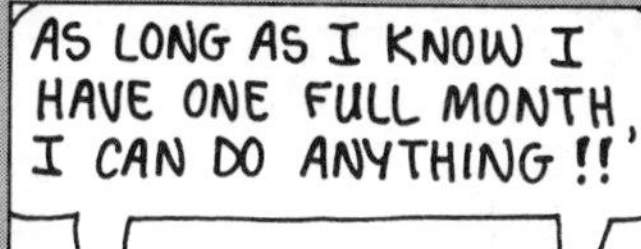
AS LONG AS I KNOW I HAVE ONE FULL MONTH, I CAN DO ANYTHING!!

MEMO-RIAL DAY IS IN THREE WEEKS.
WE'LL HAVE THE PIE.
NO ONE CAN EVER FAULT US FOR NOT STICKING TO OUR SYSTEM.
Guisewite

I DON'T KNOW WHAT TO DO FOR MOTHER'S DAY THIS YEAR.
ME EITHER.

IF I LET MY KIDS MAKE ME BREAKFAST, I'LL BE CLEAN-ING UP FOR WEEKS!
HA, HA! IF WE TAKE THE BABY TO A RESTAURANT, DO WE VOLUNTEER TO VACUUM WHEN WE LEAVE?
DO I HUG MY SON OR SCOLD HIM FOR PAINTING "I LOVE MOM" ON THE WALL?
WHAT TO DO! WHEW! WHO KNOWS WHAT TO DO??!

WHICH IS WORSE... ...FEARING THAT YOU'LL TURN INTO YOUR MOTHER, OR REALIZING THAT ALL YOUR FRIENDS ALREADY HAVE?
Guisewite

BATHING SUIT AD:
USED TO BE A WOMAN WITH A PERFECT BODY IN A BATHING SUIT... NOW, A WOMAN WITH A PERFECT BODY IN A BATHING SUIT ROMPING ON THE BEACH WITH HER PERFECT BABY.

BLUE JEAN AD:
USED TO BE A GORGEOUS, SKINNY WOMAN IN JEANS... ...NOW, A GORGEOUS, SKINNY WOMAN IN JEANS HOLDING HER ADORABLE BABY.
SPRING

LEISURE WEAR AD:
USED TO BE A SEXY WOMAN IN A BREEZY SUNDRESS... ...NOW, A SEXY WOMAN IN A BREEZY SUNDRESS CURLED UP WITH HER DARLING BABY.
SPRING

JUST IN CASE THE LOOK ISN'T COMPLETELY UNATTAINABLE, THEY'VE THROWN IN THE IMPOSSIBLE ACCESSORY.
Guisewite

I THOUGHT I'D HAVE A FAMILY BY NOW TOO, MOM. IT JUST HASN'T HAPPENED.
WHY?
Salad Bar

I'VE NEVER BEEN IN THE RIGHT RELATIONSHIP.
WHY?
IT'S HARD TO FIND THE RIGHT PERSON.
WHY?
I DON'T KNOW. IT JUST IS.
WHY?

STOP ASKING "WHY"! STOP ASKING "WHY"! STOP ASKING "WHY"!
WHY?
Salad Bar

AUGHH!!
...WHAT A PITY. SHE'D BE SO GOOD WITH CHILDREN...
Guisewite

YOUR FATHER AND I JUST WANT YOU TO BE HAPPY, CATHY.
THANKS, MOM.

IF YOU'RE HAPPY WITHOUT EXPERIENCING THE JOY OF PARENTHOOD THAT WE HAVE, THEN WE'RE HAPPY, TOO.
THANKS, MOM.

HOWEVER, IN CASE YOU'RE JUST SAYING YOU'RE HAPPY WHEN YOU'RE NOT REALLY HAPPY AT ALL, FLO'S NEPHEW WAS JUST DUMPED BY HIS GIRLFRIEND AND COULD BE A HOT PROSPECT...

WHAT COINCIDENCE THAT THE UMBILICAL CORD IS LOCATED SO CLOSE TO THE STOMACH.
Guisewite

WHY WASN'T I TOLD THAT IF I THREW MYSELF INTO MY CAREER I MIGHT RUN OUT OF TIME TO HAVE CHILDREN ??
I BELIEVE I MENTIONED THAT ON EACH OF YOUR LAST TEN BIRTHDAYS, CATHY.

WHY WASN'T I TOLD TO GET OUT OF RELATIONSHIPS THAT WEREN'T WORKING AND INTO ONE THAT MIGHT GO SOMEWHERE ??!
I MADE THAT POINT IN EVERY SINGLE WEEKLY PHONE CALL.

WHY WASN'T I TOLD BY SOMEONE WHO ISN'T MY MOTHER ??!

GOODBYE, TERRIBLE TWO'S. HELLO, REALLY ICKY THIRTIES.

SHE DREAMED ABOUT HAVING ME FROM THE TIME SHE WAS A LITTLE GIRL... SHE ADORED ME BEFORE I WAS EVEN CONCEIVED...

FROM THE SECOND I WAS BORN, EVERY MOMENT OF HER LIFE HAS BEEN FOCUSED ON ME... SHE LOVES ME AS DEEPLY AND COMPLETELY AS ANYONE HAS EVER LOVED ANYONE SINCE THE BEGINNING OF TIME...

AND NOW I SIMPLY HAVE TO FIND A MOTHER'S DAY GIFT THAT NOT ONLY THANKS MOM FOR A LIFE OF SELFLESS GIVING, BUT REASSURES HER THAT THE BOND SHE SO LOVINGLY NURTURED BETWEEN US WILL GO ON FOREVER.
Mall

DO YOU HAVE ANY GRANDCHILDREN I CAN RENT ?
MOTHER'S DAY GIFTS

WHAT HAPPENED, CHARLENE ? I WAS YOUNG... I WAS EVEN SORT OF CUTE... I USED UP ALL MY GOOD YEARS IN THIS STUPID OFFICE...

NOW I'M OLD AND PAST MY PRIME, AND NOW I HAVE TO LOOK FOR A HUSBAND AND FATHER OF MY CHILDREN ?? NOW, WHEN I'M WRINKLED AND FLABBY AND SET IN MY WAYS ?? NOW I'M SUPPOSED TO FIND MY PRINCE CHARMING ??

FIVE MORE MINUTES OF GOOD SKIN TONE JUST SLIPPED AWAY.
AACK!!
EXIT

IF I CAN'T PUT HER OUT OF HER MISERY, AT LEAST I CAN PUT MYSELF OUT OF MINE.

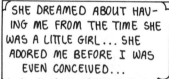

ARE YOU AVAILABLE?
YES!
OPEN-MINDED?
YES!
CONFIDENT?
YES!
INTERESTING?
YES!
Quiz

WILLING TO GIVE?
YES!
WILLING TO SHARE?
YES!
WILLING TO TRY?
YES!
WILLING TO LEARN?
YES!
WILLING TO RISK?
YES!
Quiz

DO YOU EVER LEAVE YOUR HOME EXCEPT TO DRIVE TO THE OFFICE?
NO.
Quiz

YOU'RE HOPELESS.
ONLY IN DATING ARE ALL OTHER QUALIFICATIONS OBLITERATED BY ONE WRONG ANSWER.
Guisewite

I HAD SUCH A GREAT TALK WITH MY MOM THIS MORNING!
YOU HAD A GREAT TALK WITH YOUR MOM??

SURE! ISN'T IT A RELIEF TO HAVE ALL THAT MOTHER-DAUGHTER STUFF BEHIND US?? WE HAVE GREAT TALKS EVERY DAY!
YOU HAVE GREAT TALKS EVERY DAY??

HI, MOM...
...NO, WAIT... DON'T GET DAD...
...NO, IT'S NOT "FEMALE TROUBLE"...
...WAIT...MOM! NEVER MIND! I'LL CALL LATER!

WE DON'T HAVE GREAT TALKS EVERY DAY, BUT WE HAVE PARTIALLY DECENT CONVERSATION FRAGMENTS FAIRLY OFTEN!!
Guisewite

HERE I AM, THE NO-NONSENSE EXECUTIVE IN MY NEW ULTRA-CHIC POWER SUIT...

HERE I AM, THE SULTRY TEMPTRESS IN MY NEW SPANDEX SKIRT AND BUSTIER...

HERE I AM, THE NURTURING EARTH MOTHER IN MY NEW FLOWY GARDEN FROCK...

I GOT A LIFE; HOWEVER, NOW I'D LIKE TO RETURN IT AND HAVE THE CASH.
Boutique
Guisewite

IN THE '70s, A "DIET PLATE" WAS A FRIED BEEF PATTY AND A BIG SCOOP OF COTTAGE CHEESE... REMEMBER??
MENU LITE
MENU LITE
MENU LITE
CARBOHY-DRATES WERE FOR-BIDDEN!
NOODLES WERE THE ENEMY!
ONE SLICE OF BREAD WOULD DESTROY THE DIET!
MENU LITE
WE KNEW NOTH-ING!
NOTH-ING AT ALL!
WE DID THE EXACT OPPOSITE OF WHAT'S NECESSARY TO LOSE WEIGHT!!
...OF COURSE, WE WERE ALL TEN POUNDS THINNER THEN...
PASS ME A MULTI-GRAIN, FAT-FREE CRACKER.
CURSES ON HISTORI-CAL PER-SPECTIVE.
MENU LITE
MENU LITE
MENU LITE
GUISEWITE

I'M KIND OF BUSY, MOM...
OF COURSE YOU ARE, SWEETIE. YOU'RE JAMMING YOUR LIFE FULL OF STRESS SO YOU WON'T FEEL LONELY.

WHAT?
IT'S CLASSIC! YOU IMBUE MEANINGLESS TASKS WITH LIFE-CONSUMING IMPORTANCE SO YOU WON'T HAVE TIME TO NOTICE WHAT YOU DON'T HAVE... YOU'RE SUBCONSCIOUSLY REPLACING A HUSBAND AND CHILDREN WITH A STATE OF SELF-INDUCED CHAOS!

YOU, ON THE OTHER HAND, HAVE A LITTLE TOO MUCH TIME ON YOUR HANDS, MOTHER.
WELL, THAT'S WHAT MAKES US SUCH A GREAT COMBINATION, ISN'T IT?

YOU'RE HERE WHEN I'M TIRED AND CRANKY... HERE WHEN I'M BUSY AND PREOCCUPIED...

YOU'RE HERE WHEN I CRY, HERE WHEN I SCREAM, HERE WHEN I RANT AND RAVE... YOU'RE HERE AT MY BEST, AND HERE AT MY ABSOLUTE, POSITIVE WORST...

YOU ARE THE DEFINITION OF LOVE ITSELF!

I CAN'T REACH THE DOORKNOB.

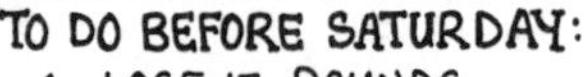
TO DO BEFORE SATURDAY:

1. LOSE 17 POUNDS.
2. TONE AND SHAPE ALL MUSCLE GROUPS.
3. BUY SWIMSUIT.

TO DO BEFORE SATURDAY:
1. LOSE 19 POUNDS.
2. TONE AND SHAPE ALL MUSCLE GROUPS.
3. BUY SWIMSUIT.

HI, CATHY. DID YOU SEE THE...
WHAT NOW?? WHAT NEXT??
EPTION

HAS OLIVE OIL BEEN RE-CLASSIFIED AS A POLYUN-SATURATE NOW THAT I'M DUMPING IT ON EVERYTHING I EAT?? HAVE THEY FOUND A WAY TO MAKE ME FEEL GUILTY ABOUT SKIM MILK, TOO??

DOES IT TURN OUT THAT LETTUCE RELEASES AN ENZYME THAT TURNS DIET SODA INTO CELLULITE ??!??

LET ME AT IT! LET ME SEE!!
SAY WHAT THEY WILL ABOUT COM-PUTERS TAKING OVER, WE NEVER LOSE OUR PASSION FOR THE MORN-ING PAPER...
RECEPTION

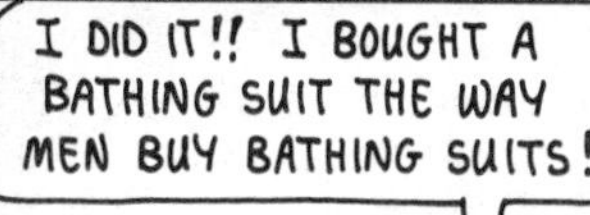
I DID IT!! I BOUGHT A BATHING SUIT THE WAY MEN BUY BATHING SUITS!

I RAN INTO THE STORE, GRABBED THE FIRST SUIT I SAW, PAID, AND RAN OUT! THE WHOLE EVENT TOOK 35 SECONDS WITHOUT ONE SPECK OF EMOTIONAL DISTRESS!!

BRAVO, CATHY! WHERE IS IT??
STUFFED IN THE TRUNK OF MY CAR, WHERE IT WILL STAY UNTIL I DRIVE TO A BRANCH OF THE SAME STORE IN A DIFFERENT COUNTY AND BEG FOR MY MONEY BACK.
OF COURSE, MEN ACTU-ALLY WEAR THE SUITS THEY BUY...
WE CAN VISIT THEIR PLANET, BUT WE CAN'T REALLY SURVIVE IN THEIR UNIVERSE.

EVERY YEAR I AGONIZE OVER SHOPPING FOR A BATH-ING SUIT, AND FOR WHAT??
SWIM WEAR

I DON'T PLAN TO GO SWIM-MING! I'M NOT GOING TO LIE IN THE SUN! WHY DO I NEED A BATHING SUIT?? HAH! I HEREBY FREE MY-SELF FROM EVER OWNING ANOTHER BATHING SUIT!!

AACK! MY MOTHER'S BODY, AND NOW MY MOTHER'S RA-TIONALIZATION PROCESS!!
WAIT UP! MY MOM AND I ARE RIGHT BEHIND YOU!

YOU HAVE A BATHING SUIT ON AND YOU'RE LOOKING IN THE MIRROR, CATHY??
YES, CHARLENE!

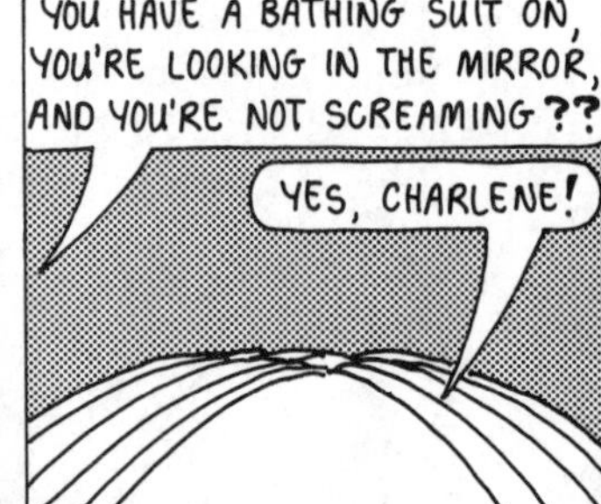
YOU HAVE A BATHING SUIT ON, YOU'RE LOOKING IN THE MIRROR, AND YOU'RE NOT SCREAMING??
YES, CHARLENE!

IS YOUR FACE PLASTERED AGAINST THE MIRROR SO YOU CAN'T SEE ANYTHING BUT THE BLUR OF YOUR OWN EYEBALLS?
YES, CHARLENE.

SORRY. DOESN'T COUNT.
THE SUPPORT GROUP GIVETH, AND THE SUPPORT GROUP TAKETH AWAY.
GUISEWITE

I CAN'T GO OUTSIDE LIKE THIS! I LOOK LIKE I'M WEARING MY UNDERWEAR!

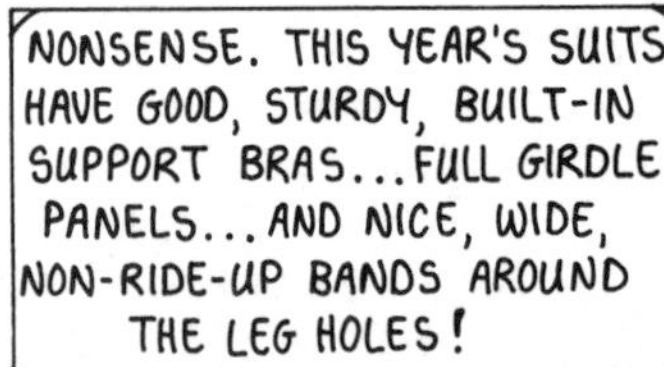
NONSENSE. THIS YEAR'S SUITS HAVE GOOD, STURDY, BUILT-IN SUPPORT BRAS...FULL GIRDLE PANELS...AND NICE, WIDE, NON-RIDE-UP BANDS AROUND THE LEG HOLES!

YOU DON'T LOOK LIKE YOU'RE WEARING YOUR UNDERWEAR!!

I LOOK LIKE I'M WEARING MY MOTHER'S UNDERWEAR!!
THE THANKS WE GET FOR TRYING TO BRING OUR CUSTOMERS INTO THE FUTURE...

SWIMWEAR SHOPPING
STAGE 1
I WANT A BATHING SUIT THAT'S FABULOUS-LOOKING, SEXY, FLIRTY AND FUN!
1

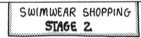

SWIMWEAR SHOPPING
STAGE 2
I WANT A BATHING SUIT THAT'S ATTRACTIVE AND FITS MY LIFE AND PERSONALITY.
1

SWIMWEAR SHOPPING
STAGE 3
I WANT SOMETHING THAT'S NOT GROSS! I'LL CONSIDER ANYTHING THAT ISN'T GROSS!!
1

ONCE AGAIN, THE QUEST FOR A BATHING SUIT PARALLELS THE SEARCH FOR A DATE.
1
OK. FINE. A LITTLE GROSS, BUT NOT REALLY, REALLY GROSS...
GUISEWITE

THE SWIM-WEAR MAKE-OVER

BEFORE

AFTER
LIPS
THIGH CREME
MAKE-UP
THIGH CREME
MAKE-UP
MOUSSE
SPRAY
GEL
COLOR
SCRUB
THIGH CREME
SMOOTHER
SKIN TONER
NAILS
THIGH CREME
MAKE-UP
BUFF BUFF BUFF
WRINKLE BAN
FAKE TAN
EYES
THIGH CREME
FAKE TAN

LATER THAT NIGHT
COOKIES

THE DAYS OF SKIMPY SWIM-WEAR ARE GONE, AND WITH THEM, WE BID A HAPPY FAREWELL TO INSECURITY AND SELF-CONSCIOUSNESS!
THE GLAMOUR SUIT

SEE? STYLES ARE MORE SOPHISTICATED...CUTS ARE MORE MODEST... EVEN THE COLORS ARE MORE DEMURE...

AS YOU LOUNGE BY THE POOL THIS SUMMER, YOU'LL BE THE PICTURE OF GLAMOUR AND ELEGANCE...JUST MAKE SURE YOU WEAR LOTS OF PROTECTION ON YOUR FACE!

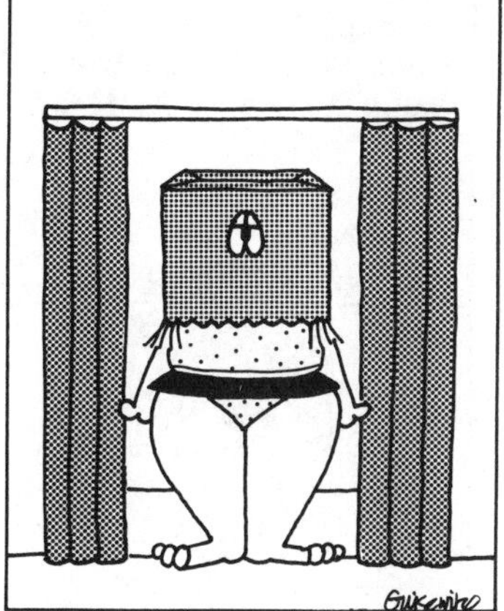

BLEAH TO THE ADS THAT MAKE ME FEEL LIKE A FAILURE IF I DON'T MEASURE UP TO SOME EMACIATED SUPERMODEL!

BLEAH TO THE IMAGES THAT CREATE A COMPLETELY UNREALISTIC "NORM" FOR THE FEMALE FIGURE! AND BLEAH, BLEAH, BLEAH TO THE WHOLE MISERABLE SOCIETY THAT MEASURES VALUE AS A HUMAN BEING BY BODY SIZE!!

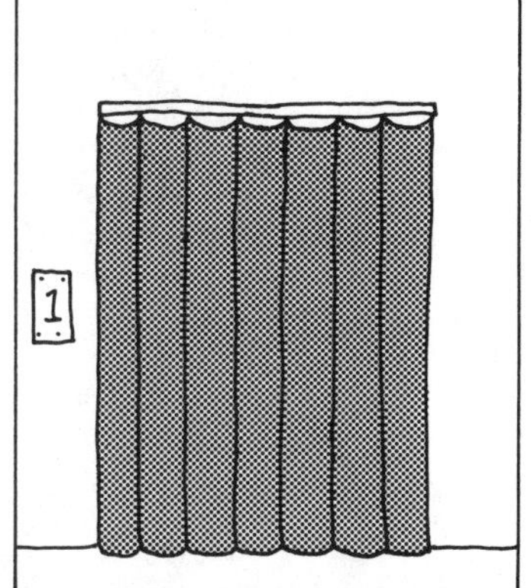
1

MEN WILL JUST HAVE TO BE ATTRACTED BY MY CHARMING PERSONALITY!!
1

THE PADDED, PUSH-UP BATHING SUIT GIVES THE ILLUSION OF A VOLUPTUOUS BUST... BUT **THEN** WHAT??

I COULD WEAR LINGERIE THAT DUPLICATES THE EFFECT THE REST OF THE TIME... ...BUT **THEN** WHAT?

HOW CAN I BUY A SUIT THAT WILL EVENTUALLY FORCE ME TO REVEAL MYSELF A FRAUD... ...BUT HOW CAN I **NOT** BUY A SUIT THAT, FOR THE FIRST TIME IN MY LIFE, GIVES ME A CHEST???

DO YOU WANT TO TAKE THAT?
NO, BUT I WANT TO COME VISIT IT.
SWIM

DECEMBER 31, 1994: HURLED INTO MY CLOSET AND CREATED A LAST-MINUTE NEW YEAR'S EVE OUTFIT OUT OF A WRINKLED NIGHTIE, A PAIR OF OLD LEGGINGS, AND PART OF A HALLOWEEN COSTUME.

MARCH 21, 1995: RAN INTO THE BATHROOM AND DID A FULL MAKEOVER IN THE 14 SECONDS BETWEEN WHEN THE DOORBELL RANG AND I GREETED MY SURPRISE DINNER GUEST.

JUNE 9, 1995: ENTERED A DRESSING ROOM WITH 25 SWIMSUITS, UNDRESSED UNDER FLUORESCENT LIGHTS, HAD A FULL BREAKDOWN, RECOVERED, AND EMERGED SEVEN MINUTES LATER WITH A WHOLE NEW REASON TO LIVE.

ALL OF MY REALLY BIG VICTORIES HAPPEN IN LITTLE TINY ROOMS.

I SURVIVED SWIMWEAR SHOPPING!

I FACED MY PERSONAL DEMONS... ROSE ABOVE MY INSECURITIES... PERSEVERED WHEN I FELT LIKE QUITTING... MADE PEACE WITH MY PAST... RALLIED FOR THE FUTURE... AND LIBERATED MYSELF FROM ALL EGO GARBAGE!!

IT TOOK 19 HOURS OVER A FIVE-DAY PERIOD, BUT I EMERGED WITH A $78 SWIMSUIT AND A SENSE OF ACCOMPLISHMENT THAT IS A BUILDING BLOCK OF STRENGTH UPON WHICH I CAN DRAW TO HELP COPE WITH ALL FUTURE IMPOSSIBLE SITUATIONS!!

HUH?
MEN, FOR INSTANCE.
WHO THOUGHT THE NEXT CHALLENGE WOULD COME SO QUICKLY...

I CAN'T TAKE THE RED EYE TO MILWAUKEE BECAUSE I NEED TO WEAR THE TAUPE SUIT MY FIRST DAY THERE.
WHAT??
PLANE TICKET

IF I DON'T GET A FULL NIGHT'S SLEEP, I'LL WAKE UP ONE SIZE TOO BIG FOR THE BOTTOM HALF OF THE SUIT.
WHAT??
PLANE TICKET

FAT CELLS NEED EIGHT FULL HOURS OF SLEEP TO RELAX AND DISPERSE, WHICH IS WHY WE WEIGH LESS IN THE MORNING!... I'M ALREADY PACKING THE TAUPE SUIT TO ACCOMMODATE AIRPLANE BLOAT... I'M NOT GOING UP ANOTHER SIZE FOR SLEEP DEPRIVATION!!
WHAT??

FOR ALL THE TIME MEN SPEND LOOKING AT WOMEN'S BODIES, THEY KNOW ABSOLUTELY NOTHING ABOUT THEM.
Guisewite

I'M BEAUTIFUL, BRIGHT, CHARMING, TALENTED AND READY TO SHARE MY LIFE WITH SOMEONE, CHARLENE!
RECEPTION

I WANT TO DREAM WITH SOMEONE... PLAN WITH SOMEONE... I WANT TO BE THERE FOR SOMEONE, AND I WANT SOMEONE TO BE THERE FOR ME!

MY HUSBAND HAS A REALLY CUTE FRIEND WHO...
AACK!! A FIX-UP?? ARE YOU OUT OF YOUR MIND?? NO FIX-UPS!!

I'M READY TO BE MARRIED. I'M NOT READY TO DATE.
RECEPTION
Guisewite

IMAGINE SITTING IN A DARK, COZY ROOM FILLED WITH IMPORTANT BUSINESSMEN WHO HAVE NOTHING TO DO FOR FOUR HOURS BUT STRIKE UP A CONVERSATION WITH YOU!

IMAGINE PUSHING A LITTLE BUTTON ON YOUR CHAIR TO HAVE SOMEONE BRING YOU A PILLOW OR A NICE, COLD DRINK!

IMAGINE SOARING ABOVE YOUR TROUBLES AND THEN BEING WHISKED AWAY BY AN EXOTIC FOREIGN DRIVER!
...RED EYE... ECONOMY CLASS... SHUTTLE BUS....

BLEAH! BUSINESS TRIP! BUSINESS TRIP! BUSINESS TRIP!
IMAGINE MENTIONING SHE HAS TO STAY OVER ON A SATURDAY SO WE COULD GET THE CHEAP RATE.

IT IS WITH PRIDE THAT I ANNOUNCE OUR CORPORATE DECISION TO JOIN THE NATIONWIDE RETURN TO WHOLESOME VALUES, SOLID MORALS AND SIMPLER TIMES!

AS A FIRST SYMBOLIC GESTURE, I'VE ASKED CATHY TO VOLUNTARILY DONATE HER BUSINESS TRIP FREQUENT FLIER MILES TO THE COMPANY POOL, SO WE MAY ALL SHARE IN THE FUTURE SAVINGS!

INSTEAD OF HOARDING MILES, CATHY WILL BE EARNING THE RICHER REWARD OF KNOWING SHE HAS OUR HEARTFELT THANKS!...IN SHORT, GOODBYE, BONUS POINTS. HELLO, BROWNIE POINTS!

JUST LIKE THE GOOD OLD DAYS...CONFETTI FOLLOWED BY A LITTLE PARADE....
Guisewite

LET ME SEE IF I UNDERSTAND... TO SAVE MONEY FOR THE COMPANY, I'M FLYING ON THE CHEAPEST RATE IN THE SMALLEST SEAT ON THE WORST AIRLINE ON A NO-FRILLS, RED EYE FLIGHT...

I'M DESERTING MY DOG, UPSETTING MY SCHEDULE, RISKING MY LIFE, CANCELING ALL MY PLANS AND SACRIFICING THREE EVENINGS AND A WEEKEND, NOT TO MENTION FOUR DAYS OF PREPARATION AND RECOVERY TIME...

AND THEN, WHEN IT'S ALL DONE, I'M GIVING THE FREQUENT FLIER MILES I WAS SAVING FOR MY VACATION BACK TO THE COMPANY SO THE NEXT ICKY BUSINESS TRIP CAN BE EVEN CHEAPER ??!

EXCELLENT! YOU HAVE AN EXCELLENT GRASP OF THE PROGRAM!!
TAKE THE COMPLIMENT. IT'S ALL WE HAVE LEFT.
Guisewite

I CAN'T LEAVE TOWN ON A BUSINESS TRIP BECAUSE I'VE SENT OUT PSYCHIC VIBES THAT I'M EMOTIONALLY READY TO MEET SOMEONE NEW.

I CAN'T LEAVE TOWN BECAUSE I'VE SUMMONED THE FORCES OF THE UNIVERSE TO SEND A NEW LOVE MY WAY AND HE MIGHT SHOW UP WHILE I'M GONE! HE MIGHT BE ON HIS WAY RIGHT NOW! I CANNOT LEAVE TOWN UNTIL HE APPEARS, AND THAT IS THE END OF THAT!

I HAVE TO LEAVE TOWN.
PERSONNEL ISSUES ALWAYS RESOLVE THEMSELVES IF YOU LET THEM.
Guisewite

IN "FRENCH KISS," SHE MET HER SWEETHEART ON A PLANE. MAYBE YOU'LL MEET SOMEONE ON THE PLANE!

BUT IN "THE BRIDGES OF MADISON COUNTY," SHE MET HIM AT HOME. YOU NEED TO STAY HOME!

BUT IN "FRENCH KISS," SHE HAD TO FLY TO FIND TRUE LOVE!
BUT IN "THE BRIDGES OF MADISON COUNTY," TRUE LOVE FOUND HER ON THE GROUND!

IT'S A SIGN! TAKE THE BUSINESS TRIP!
NO! IT'S AN OMEN! REFUSE TO GO!
NO! FLY!
NO! STAY!
NO! FLY!
NO! STAY!

ANOTHER TEN YEARS OF CAREER STRATEGIZING WIPED OUT BY THE SUMMER ROMANCE MOVIES.
Guisewite

YOUR BIG PRESENTATION IN MILWAUKEE WILL BE FRIDAY, BUT, OF COURSE, IT'S DRESS-DOWN FRIDAY, SO GO CASUAL.

...BUT NOT **TOO** CASUAL SINCE THEIR OFFICE MIGHT BE THE DRESSY-CASUAL TYPE... BUT NOT **TOO** DRESSY SINCE THEY MIGHT BE THE CASUAL-CASUAL TYPE....

WHY NOT JUST PACK FIVE DIFFERENT OUTFITS, HIDE IN A CAB OUTSIDE THEIR OFFICE, PEEK AT WHAT EVERYONE'S WEARING AS THEY WALK IN, AND CHANGE CLOTHES ACCORDINGLY IN THE BACK OF THE CAB?

WHAT A PROFESSIONAL!
GOOD TO KNOW MY WHOLE SOCIAL LIFE HASN'T BEEN A COMPLETE WASTE.
Guisewite

MARKETING PLAN TO FINISH: I'LL DO IT ON THE PLANE...
TO TAKE

FINANCIAL PROJECTIONS TO CALCULATE: I'LL DO IT ON THE PLANE... BACKGROUND MATERIAL TO GO OVER: I'LL DO IT ON THE PLANE...
TO TAKE

CHRISTMAS THANK YOU NOTES TO WRITE... ADDRESS BOOK TO REDO... FILES TO ORGANIZE... FOUR MONTHS OF NEWSPAPERS TO READ... I'LL DO IT ON THE PLANE! **I'LL DO IT ALL ON THE PLANE!!!**

READY TO MAKE YOUR SEAT SELECTION?
YES. I'LL TAKE SEAT NUMBER 8 THROUGH SEAT NUMBER 37.
TO TAKE
Guisewite

BETTER TO EAT A FROZEN YOGURT ON THE GROUND THAN WAIT FOR THE AIRPLANE MEAL AND BE SO HUNGRY I EAT THE WHOLE THING...
AIRPORT
YOGURT

BETTER TO EAT A HAMBURGER AND FRIES ON THE GROUND THAN WAIT FOR THE AIRPLANE MEAL AND BE SO HUNGRY I EAT THE WHOLE THING...
AIRPORT
HAMBURGER

BETTER TO EAT A BLUEBERRY MUFFIN, SOFT PRETZEL, SLICE OF PIZZA AND SMALL BAG OF POPCORN ON THE GROUND THAN WAIT FOR THE AIRPLANE MEAL AND BE SO HUNGRY I EAT THE WHOLE THING....
POP CORN

HOW MANY MORE MINUTES UNTIL THE MEAL IS SERVED?!!

THE HOTEL HEALTH CLUB HAS MACHINES AND TRAINERS AVAILABLE 24 HOURS A DAY... ...THERE ARE LOW-FAT OPTIONS FOR ALL ROOM SERVICE ITEMS...
Registration

YOUR ROOM IS EQUIPPED WITH A BATHROOM SCALE, A SEWING KIT, AN IRON, A STACK OF STATIONERY FOR ALL THOSE NOTES YOU'VE BEEN MEANING TO WRITE, AND A LITTLE RE-FRIGERATOR FULL OF FAT-TENING SNACKS!

IT'S OUR LITTLE WAY OF MAKING SURE OUR GUESTS FEEL RIGHT AT HOME!

AACK! FOUR STAR GUILT!!
YOUR IN-ROOM VOICE MAIL ALREADY HAS THREE MES-SAGES WAITING FROM YOUR MOTHER.
Registration
Guisewite

HOW MANY IN YOUR PARTY?
ONE. THERE'S ONE OF ME IN MY PARTY!
BELL CAPTAIN

THIS IS LUGGAGE FOR **ONE**! THIS IS THE EXACT AMOUNT OF LUGGAGE REQUIRED BY **ONE** WOMAN FOR A THREE-DAY TRIP!!
BELL CAPTAIN

I WILL NEVER AGAIN APOLO-GIZE FOR BEING ONE! I'M PROUD TO BE ONE, AND PROUD OF ALL THAT GOES WITH IT!

ROOM SERVICE FOR HOW MANY?
TWO.
Guisewite

A FEW CLOTHES... A FEW TOILETRIES... WHAT ELSE DO I REALLY NEED BESIDES WHAT'S IN THIS HOTEL ROOM?

WHY HAVE I LET LIFE GET SO COMPLICATED?? AS SOON AS I GO HOME, I'LL CLEAR OUT MY CLOSETS! ELIMINATE ALL PILES OF PAPER!

I'LL VISIT MUSEUMS! ATTEND THE BALLET! WRITE LETTERS TO LOVED ONES! THROW DIN-NER PARTIES! SPEND QUALI-TY TIME WITH MY DOG AND LIVE A MORE BALANCED, EN-RICHING, STRESS-FREE LIFE!

...INCREDIBLE HOW EFFICIENT I BECOME WHEN I'M 1300 MILES AWAY FROM MY LIFE.
Guisewite

I NEED A WAKE-UP CALL FOR 6:00AM SHARP!
FINE. 6:00AM.
BUT I MIGHT GO BACK TO SLEEP. I NEED A BACKUP CALL AT 6:05.
BACKUP CALL AT 6:05.

IF I SOUND GROGGY, SCREAM IN MY EAR UNTIL I CON- VINCE YOU I'M STANDING UP.
SCREAM AT 6:07.
I ABSOLUTELY, POSITIVELY MUST BE AWAKE BY 6:07 AM!
YOU'LL BE WIDE AWAKE BY 6:07AM!

TO WHOM DO I SPEAK ABOUT FALLING ASLEEP?

WHAT IF I OVERSLEEP AND MISS THE MEETING?
WHAT IF MY PRESENTA- TION'S NOT GOOD ENOUGH?
WHAT IF I MAKE A FOOL OF MYSELF?
WHAT IF I GET FIRED?

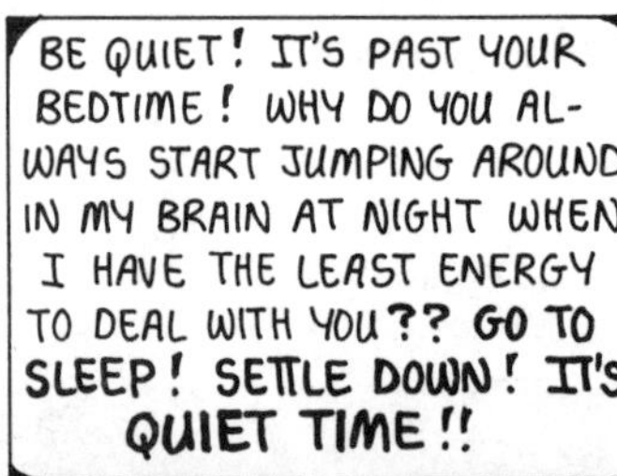
BE QUIET! IT'S PAST YOUR BEDTIME! WHY DO YOU AL- WAYS START JUMPING AROUND IN MY BRAIN AT NIGHT WHEN I HAVE THE LEAST ENERGY TO DEAL WITH YOU?? GO TO SLEEP! SETTLE DOWN! IT'S QUIET TIME!!

WHAT IF MY HAIR DRIER DOESN'T WORK IN THE MORNING?
WHAT IF I BROUGHT THE WRONG PRESENTATION?
WHAT IF I FLEW TO THE WRONG CITY?
WHAT IF I PANIC AND START BABBLING IN THE MEETING?

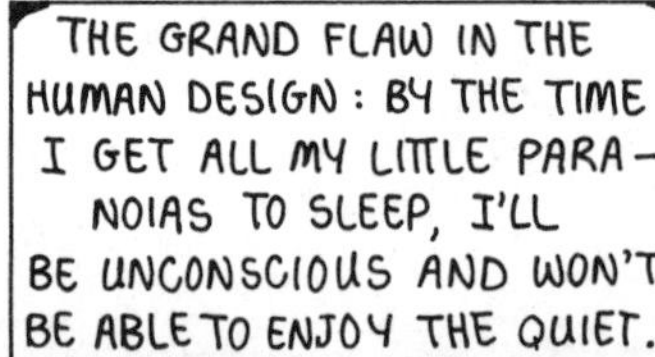
THE GRAND FLAW IN THE HUMAN DESIGN: BY THE TIME I GET ALL MY LITTLE PARA- NOIAS TO SLEEP, I'LL BE UNCONSCIOUS AND WON'T BE ABLE TO ENJOY THE QUIET.

I CAN'T SLEEP. THE ROOM'S TOO DARK... I CAN'T SLEEP. THE ROOM'S TOO BRIGHT... I CAN'T SLEEP. THE ROOM'S TOO HOT. NOW IT'S TOO COLD. THE COVERS ARE TOO THICK. THE BED'S TOO HARD. THE PIL- LOWS ARE TOO BOUNCY.

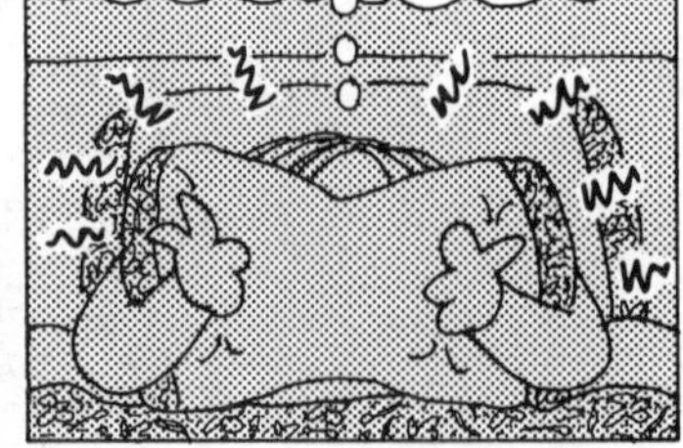
THE AIR CONDITIONER'S TOO LOUD. THE CLOCK'S TOO LOUD. THE SINK'S TOO LOUD. THE WALLPAPER'S TOO LOUD. THE DUST IS TOO LOUD. THE MI- CROSCOPIC FIBERS OF THE CARPET ARE TOO LOUD...

BE QUIET! I HAVE A BIG MEETING TOMORROW! I NEED MY SLEEP! EVERY- ONE BE QUIET!

I CAN'T SLEEP. IT'S TOO QUIET.

ONE PRE-FLIGHT PANIC SNACK AT AIRPORT FUDGE SHOPPE: **675 CALORIES.**
FOUR BAGS OF NUTS WITH FOUR BEVERAGES PRECEDING FOUR AIRPLANE MEALS: **4200 CALORIES.**
TRIP RECEIPTS

ONE PRE-PRESENTATION ANXIETY FLING WITH HOTEL ROOM MINI BAR: **1144 CALORIES.**
32 NERVOUS-ENERGY BREATH MINTS: **195 CALORIES.**
THREE FOUR-HOUR CLIENT DINNERS: **5300 CALORIES.**

TWO SELF-PITY ROOM SERVICE EPISODES: **1900 CALORIES.**
ONE EXHAUSTION-INDUCED-LAPSE-OF-JUDGMENT STOP AT NEWSSTAND CANDY COUNTER: **837 CALORIES.**

I'LL HAND MY BONUS MILES OVER TO THE COMPANY, BUT YOU'LL ALSO HAVE TO TAKE OVER THE BONUS FAT THAT CAME WITH THEM.
Guisewite

COFFEE...
...I NEED COFFEE IMMEDIATELY...
WE'LL HAVE THAT UP FOR YOU IN 45 MINUTES.

I ONLY GOT A HALF-HOUR OF SLEEP... I'M BEGGING YOU! I NEED COFFEE NOW!
WE'LL HAVE THAT UP FOR YOU IN 45 MINUTES.

BRING ME MY COFFEE! BRING ME MY COFFEE! BRING ME MY COFFEE!
WE'LL HAVE THAT UP FOR YOU IN 45 MINUTES.

ANOTHER ALL-POWERFUL BUSINESS TRAVELER LEVELED BY THE ALMIGHTY ROOM-SERVICE ORDER-TAKER.
I'LL PAY EXTRA.
OOPS. A BIG WAFFLE ORDER JUST CAME IN. YOUR COFFEE WILL BE UP IN AN HOUR AND A HALF.
Guisewite

WHAT A POWERFUL PRESENTATION, CATHY!
I WAS CRANKY BECAUSE I DIDN'T GET MY COFFEE THIS MORNING.

YOU NAILED EVERY ATTACK WITH A RAZOR-SHARP COUNTERATTACK!
I WAS TOO TIRED TO BE PLEASANT.

YOU SPOKE WITH SUCH POINTED EFFICIENCY! WE WERE RIVETED!
I HAD TO GET THROUGH MY SPEECH AND SIT DOWN BEFORE ANYONE NOTICED MY SUIT WAS SCORCHED.

BRAVO! BRAVO!
MY WINNING FORMULA: LOUSY ROOM SERVICE, INSOMNIA AND A BROKEN IRON.
Guisewite

THE POWERFULLY ELEGANT & ALLURING FEMALE BUSINESS TRAVELLER
CHIC HAT
SMOLDERING EYE MAKEUP
SEXY HAIR
STRONG, YET POUTY LIPS
PEEK-A-BOO JEWELRY
POWER LINGERIE
SAUCY YET SOPHISTICATED BUSTIER
BODY-MOLDING JACKET
COY HANDBAG
TANTALIZINGLY CURVY SKIRT
NAKED HOSE
ULTRA-GLAMOROUS STRAPPY STILETTO HEELS
SIREN-RED TOENAILS
PC

THE MALE RESPONSE
WOW! IS THAT A LAPTOP??
GATE 23
PC

WELCOME BACK, CATHY! HERE ARE YOUR PHONE MESSAGES!
THAT'S IT??
RECEPTION

DID ANYONE CALL AND NOT LEAVE A MESSAGE?? AND IF SO, WAS IT A MAN?? AND IF SO, DID YOU RECOGNIZE THE VOICE?? AND IF SO, WERE THERE ANY SUBTLE NUANCES THAT GAVE A CLUE REGARDING HIS EMOTIONAL STATE??

I DON'T KNOW. I WAS OUT SICK TWO DAYS.
AHAH! CALL THE TEMP SERVICE! TRACK DOWN AND INTERROGATE THE TEMP!!
RECEPTION

EIGHTEEN PHONE MESSAGES, AND THE ONLY ONE THAT SHOT HER INTO ACTION WAS THE ONE THAT DOESN'T EXIST.
RECEPTION

THIS IS A PICTURE OF THE HOTEL SHUTTLE BUS WHIZZING PAST ME FOR THE SIXTH TIME WITHOUT STOPPING...
PHOTOS

THIS IS A SHOT OF THE NEWSSTAND CASHIER WHO TOOK 19 MINUTES TO RING UP A PACK OF BREATH MINTS AND ALMOST MADE ME MISS MY FLIGHT...
PHOTOS

HERE'S THE 400-POUND MAN SEATED NEXT TO ME ON THE PLANE WITH MY BRIEFCASE CRUSHED UNDER HIS RIGHT FOOT... HERE'S THE $24.00 BOWL OF CEREAL I DIDN'T GET TO EAT BECAUSE IT CAME TOO LATE... HERE ARE 238 IDENTICAL BLACK SUITCASES FROM MY PLANE, NONE OF WHICH IS MINE....

THERE ARE NO TRAVEL PHOTOS SO INSPIRING AS THOSE THAT MAKE YOU THRILLED YOU'RE NOT ON A TRIP.
MY **OFFICE**!!

MONDAY AFTERNOON: THE TIDE OF PAPERS FLOWS OUT.
CATHY
TUESDAY MORNING: THE TIDE OF PAPERS FLOWS BACK IN.

CATHY
TUESDAY AFTERNOON: THE TIDE OF PAPERS FLOWS OUT.
WEDNESDAY MORNING: THE TIDE OF PAPERS FLOWS BACK IN.
CATHY

WEDNESDAY AFTERNOON: THE TIDE FLOWS OUT.
CATHY

THURSDAY MORNING: THE TIDE FLOWS BACK IN.
CATHY

HOW CAN SOMETHING SO COMFORTING IN NATURE BE SO IRRITATING IN MY OFFICE?
CATHY

THANKS FOR TAKING CARE OF ELECTRA WHILE I WAS OUT OF TOWN, MOM.
IT WAS A JOY, CATHY.

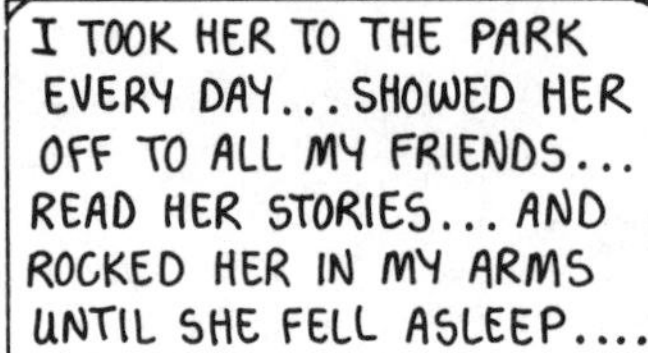
I TOOK HER TO THE PARK EVERY DAY... SHOWED HER OFF TO ALL MY FRIENDS... READ HER STORIES... AND ROCKED HER IN MY ARMS UNTIL SHE FELL ASLEEP....

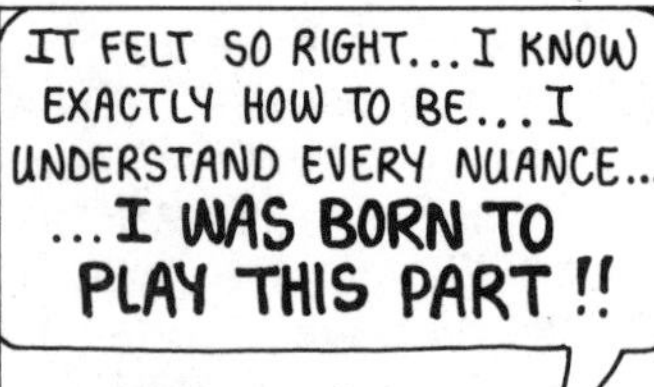
IT FELT SO RIGHT... I KNOW EXACTLY HOW TO BE... I UNDERSTAND EVERY NUANCE... ...**I WAS BORN TO PLAY THIS PART !!**

THERE'LL BE A BABY ONE OF THESE DAYS, MOM.
SO MUCH TALENT IN THE WORLD, AND NOT NEARLY ENOUGH ROLES FOR GRANDMAS.
ELECTRA

I KNOW YOU'RE ANGRY BECAUSE I WENT AWAY, ELECTRA. YOU'RE ACTING COLD AND DISTANT BECAUSE YOU'RE HURT.

PART OF YOU WANTS TO HURT ME BACK, AND PART OF YOU JUST DOESN'T WANT TO GET CLOSE BECAUSE YOU'RE AFRAID I'LL LEAVE AGAIN... I UNDERSTAND, ELECTRA! **I'M HERE FOR YOU! TALK TO ME!!**

DOG

WHAT THERAPY CAN'T SOLVE, THE PROPERLY TIMED DOG BISCUIT CAN.
DOG

A WALK? SURE, ELECTRA. I JUST NEED TO GET MY HAND WEIGHTS, TAPE PLAYER AND WATER BOTTLE...

I'D BETTER TAKE A SWEAT-SHIRT IF IT GETS COLD... A HAT IF IT GETS HOT... I NEED MY SUNGLASSES... SUNSCREEN... LIP BALM... BLISTER CREME...

...WALLET... KEYS... CELLULAR PHONE... CONTACT CASE... CON-TACT SOLUTION... EXTRA TAPES ...WATER CUP FOR YOU... HEAD-BAND... BUSINESS CARDS... CAMERA... FILM... WHISTLE...

TA DA. READY!
HUMANS: THE ORIGINAL PACK ANIMALS.

WHAT WAS THAT SALES-PERSON THINKING??

THIS ISN'T "ELEGANT AND REFINED"! IT'S RIDICULOUS! THIS ISN'T "BRAZENLY CHIC"! IT'S EXCESSIVE AND GOOFY!

NO ONE WEARS SHOES LIKE THIS TO THE OFFICE! NO ONE WEARS LITTLE HATS TO THE OFFICE! HOW COULD SHE TALK ME INTO A GETUP LIKE THIS??!!

WHY THE MALLS DON'T OPEN UNTIL WELL AFTER THE WORKERS ARE SAFELY LOCKED IN THEIR OFFICES FOR THE DAY.

OPEN UP, I TELL YOU! OPEN UP AND DEFEND YOURSELF!!
CLOSED
HOURS:

WE COULD BE BETTER FRIENDS IF YOU WOULDN'T DO THAT, MOM.
DO WHAT?
THAT THING YOU JUST DID.
WHICH THING?

YOU READ MY MIND... MENTALLY DISAGREED WITH ME... ANTICIPATED THE ARGUMENT THAT WOULD ENSUE IF YOU SPOKE UP... PLAYED OUT THE WHOLE DISCUSSION IN YOUR HEAD... DECLARED YOURSELF THE WINNER... AND LET JUST THE SLIGHTEST TRACE OF A SMUG LOOK CROSS YOUR FACE.

OH, FOR CRYING OUT LOUD! YOU DID IT AGAIN!!
GREAT TALENT CAN'T BE STIFLED.

MEXICAN?... CHINESE?... PASTA?... ITALIAN?... INDIAN? ... PIZZA?... FRENCH?... THAI? ... SALAD?... CHICKEN?....
THAI
PASTA
FREE
THAI

TOO MANY MENUS... TOO MANY CHOICES... TOO MANY DECISIONS...
TAKE OUT
FREE DELIVERY
CHINESE
INDIAN
MENU
TAKE OUT PIZZA
TAKE OUT

JUST SEND SOME FOOD! I DON'T EVEN CARE WHAT IT IS!! JUST SEND SOME FOOD OVER HERE!!
CLICK
MENU
CHINESE TAKE OUT
FREE
THAI

INCREDIBLE... IT'S BECOME EASIER TO COOK DINNER THAN TO ORDER.
FRENCH
MENU

GO FOR A WALK! GO TO THE PARK! PLAY BALL! PLAY FRISBEE! TUG-OF-WAR!

COOKIE! STEAK! FRENCH FRY! FIND STICKS! CHASE CATS!

YOU'RE READY FOR A BATH, AREN'T YOU, ELECTRA?

I LOVE HOW WE COMMUNICATE WITHOUT WORDS...

DO YOU EVER THINK ABOUT ALEX, CATHY?
ALEX? OH, NO! THAT'S OVER! LONG GONE! NO FEELINGS! NO INTEREST! IT'S OVER! FINITO! FINISHED! HA, HA! WHEW! NO!
RECEPTION

HE CALLED WHILE YOU WERE OUT.
RECEPTION

REFLEX MAKE-OVER.
NICE TO SEE YOUR BRAIN AND BODY ARE STILL FUNCTIONING INDEPENDENTLY.
RECEPTION

SHOULD I CALL ALEX BACK NOW OR CALL HIM LATER?... CALL HIM NOW OR CALL HIM LATER?... CALL HIM NOW OR CALL HIM LATER?...

IF IT WERE ANYONE BUT AN EX-BOYFRIEND, WOULD I EVEN BE THINKING ABOUT IT??... ...NO! I'D CALL WHEN IT WAS CONVENIENT! I MIGHT FORGET TO CALL! I MIGHT REMEMBER TO CALL, BUT JUST NOT FEEL LIKE TALKING TO HIM!

WHY SHOULD AN EX-BOYFRIEND BE DIFFERENT?...WHY SHOULD HE TAKE PRIORITY OVER ANYTHING?... WHY SHOULD EVEN ONE SECOND BE SPENT ON A MENTAL DEBATE???

...WELL, THAT WRAPS UP THE MORNING. WANT TO GO FOR LUNCH?
ONLY IF WE CAN SPEND IT DISCUSSING HOW PROUD I AM FOR NOT LEAPING ON THE PHONE.

IT WILL NEVER BE LIKE IT WAS THE FIRST TIME, CHARLENE...

YEAH, I KNOW, CATHY...
I WAS SO INNOCENT. SO FULL OF HOPE...

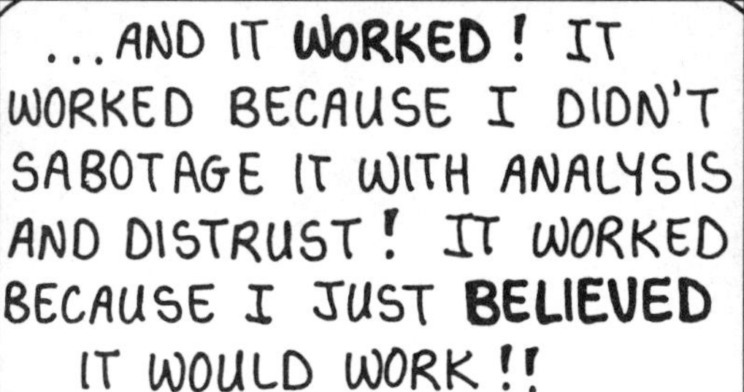
...AND IT **WORKED**! IT WORKED BECAUSE I DIDN'T SABOTAGE IT WITH ANALYSIS AND DISTRUST! IT WORKED BECAUSE I JUST **BELIEVED** IT WOULD WORK!!

FIRST LOVE?
FIRST DIET.
I'D NEVER EVEN HEARD OF TRANS-FATTY ACIDS!!

I'VE DECIDED TO CALL ALEX BACK AT 7:30 TONIGHT WHEN I KNOW I'LL GET HIS MACHINE.
YOU WANT TO LEAVE A MESSAGE?

OH, NO. I WON'T LEAVE A MESSAGE. I JUST WANT TO HEAR HIM SPEAK WHEN HE'S NOT THERE SO I CAN SQUELCH ANY POTENTIAL EMOTIONAL REACTION TO THE SOUND OF HIS VOICE.

ONCE I'VE ADJUSTED TO HIS VOICE, I'LL FORCE MYSELF TO LOOK AT CUTE PICTURES OF HIM UNTIL ALL RESPONSE IS NUMBED... THEN AND ONLY THEN WILL I RECEIVE A CALL FROM HIM AND REITERATE THAT I'M NOT INTERESTED!!

BEING A WOMAN IS LIKE HOLDING 12 FULL-TIME JOBS...
Guisewite

OK, ALEX, I'M READY! DO I HAVE ANY SECOND THOUGHTS ABOUT YOUR PROPOSAL?...NO! DO I WANT TO GIVE IT ANOTHER TRY?... ...NO! DO I WISH WE WERE STILL TOGETHER?...NO!

RING RING

HELLO?
HI, CATHY. IT'S ALEX.

WE'RE HAVING A MEMBERSHIP DRIVE AT THE GYM AND NEED TO KNOW IF YOU'RE PLANNING TO RENEW.

HAVE 5,000 YEARS OF DATING PREPARED ANY WOMAN TO DEAL WITH AN ACTUAL MAN?....NO.
Guisewite

YOU HAVEN'T COME TO THE GYM SINCE WE BROKE UP, CATHY.
I THOUGHT IT WOULD BE TOO UNCOMFORTABLE, ALEX.

I WOULDN'T BE UNCOMFORTABLE. WHY WOULD YOU BE UNCOMFORTABLE?
I'D BE UNCOMFORTABLE BECAUSE I'D THINK IT WAS UNCOMFORTABLE FOR YOU.

BUT I WOULDN'T BE UNCOMFORTABLE.
BUT I'D THINK YOU SHOULD BE UNCOMFORTABLE, AND I'D GET VERY UNCOMFORTABLE THAT YOU WEREN'T UNCOMFORTABLE, WHICH I'D PROJECT BACK ONTO YOU, MAKING YOU EXTREMELY UNCOMFORTABLE, AND THEN....

AAGH.
EVEN WHEN THERE'S NO SPARK, I CAN FAN IT INTO A FLAME.
Guisewite

IF SEEING ME AT THE GYM IS TOO MUCH LIKE A DATE, MAYBE WE COULD HAVE LUNCH SOMETIME, CATHY.
LUNCH IS TOO MUCH LIKE A DATE, ALEX.

HOW ABOUT BREAKFAST?
BREAKFAST IS TOO MUCH LIKE A DATE.
COFFEE?
COFFEE IS TOO MUCH LIKE A DATE.
I'LL JUST STOP OVER AND SAY HI SOMETIME.
STOPPING OVER IS TOO MUCH LIKE A DATE.

THERE CAN BE NO FOOD, NO BEVERAGE, NO ENTERTAIN-MENT AND NO POTENTIALLY FLIRTATIOUSLY AMBIVALENT ENCOUNTERS OF ANY KIND!

THE WORLD IS NEVER SO RIPE WITH ROMANTIC POSSIBILITY AS WHEN YOU'RE TRYING TO NOT GO OUT WITH SOMEONE.
Guisewite

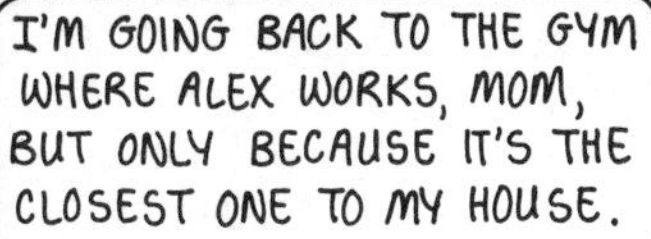
I'M GOING BACK TO THE GYM WHERE ALEX WORKS, MOM, BUT ONLY BECAUSE IT'S THE CLOSEST ONE TO MY HOUSE.

Workout

I'M OVER HIM. HE'S OVER ME. WE'RE BOTH RELIEVED IT ENDED WHEN IT DID.
Workout

THERE'S NO MEANING, NO SIGNIFICANCE, NO ULTERIOR MOTIVE, NO HIDDEN AGENDA! I'LL SIMPLY BE WORKING OUT UNDER THE SAME ROOF AS SOMEONE I ONCE DATED!

THERE SHE GOES AGAIN, TAUNTING ME WITH FALSE HOPE.
Guisewite

HI, CATHY!
UH, OH. BIG MISTAKE. BIG MISTAKE. BIG MISTAKE.
STAFF

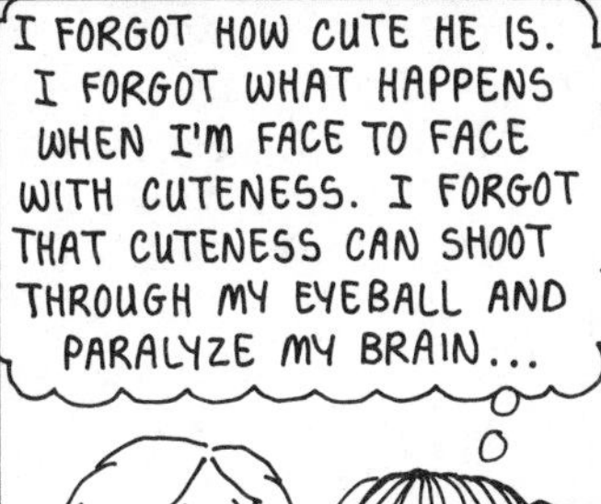
I FORGOT HOW CUTE HE IS. I FORGOT WHAT HAPPENS WHEN I'M FACE TO FACE WITH CUTENESS. I FORGOT THAT CUTENESS CAN SHOOT THROUGH MY EYEBALL AND PARALYZE MY BRAIN...

EXCUSE ME! CONTACT LENS EMERGENCY!! CONTACT LENS EMERGENCY!!
STAFF

...I NEED TO TAKE THE LENS-ES OUT SO I WON'T BE ABLE TO SEE HIM AS CLEARLY.
Guisewite

YOU LOOK GREAT, CATHY!
THANKS, ALEX.
TOWELS
GYM
STAFF

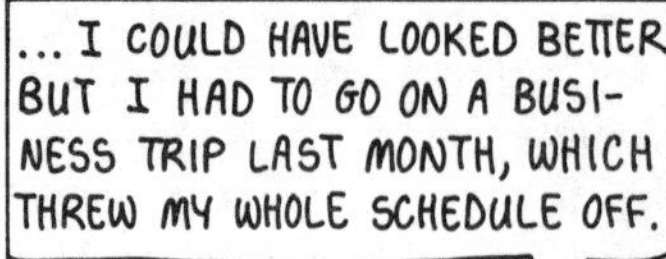
...I COULD HAVE LOOKED BETTER BUT I HAD TO GO ON A BUSINESS TRIP LAST MONTH, WHICH THREW MY WHOLE SCHEDULE OFF.

STAFF

I'D BEEN DOING SO WELL... I WAS ON A GREAT PROGRAM... IF I'D ONLY BEEN ABLE TO STAY ON MY PROGRAM FOR FOUR MORE WEEKS IN A ROW, I COULD HAVE LOOKED **INCREDIBLE** RIGHT NOW!!

UM, GEE... I'M SORRY.
WHY SETTLE FOR A COMPLIMENT WHEN YOU CAN GO FOR CONDOLENCES?
LASSES
STAFF
Guisewite

I KNOW THAT SOMEDAY I'LL MEET A WOMAN WHO LOVES TO CAMP AS MUCH AS I DO, CATHY.
HE KNOWS EXACTLY WHO HE IS AND DOESN'T TRANSFORM HIMSELF TO MATCH WHO HE'S DATING.

I WANT TO BUILD A CABIN WITH HER BY HAND AND HOME-SCHOOL OUR CHILDREN.
HE STANDS BY HIS DREAMS FOR HIMSELF, NO MATTER WHAT.

I'M REALLY GLAD I GOT TO KNOW YOU, AND HOPE YOU'LL FIND SOMEONE WONDERFUL.
HE'S THE EXACT RIGHT COMBINATION OF WARMTH, SINCERITY, AND COMPLETE ALOOFNESS.

HOW IRONIC THAT AFTER ALL THESE YEARS IT TURNS OUT THAT MEN HAVE WOMEN'S MAGAZINES BUILT INTO THEIR BRAINS.
Guisewite

SEE YOU AROUND, CATHY.
WAIT...THAT'S **IT** BETWEEN US, ALEX?
GYM

IT WAS PRETTY MUCH "IT" WHEN YOU DUMPED ME FIVE MONTHS AGO.
WELL, YES, IT WAS **PRETTY MUCH** "IT," BUT STILL MORE OF A **SPECULATIVE** "IT," SINCE WE DIDN'T KNOW HOW WE'D ADJUST TO THE REALITY OF IT BEING "IT."
GYM

IF IT'S STILL "IT" AFTER FINALLY SEEING EACH OTHER AGAIN, THEN THIS IS THE **CONFIRMING** "IT."... THE **FINAL DECREE** "IT."... THE **GRAND FINALE** "IT." **THIS IS REALLY, REALLY "IT"!**

I CAN'T TAKE IT.
MEN HAVE NO SENSE OF CEREMONY.
GYM
Gym
Guisewite

HONK HONK! I CAN'T SEE! GET OUT OF MY WAY! HONK HONK!

I MISSED MY STREET BECAUSE YOUR BIG REAR WAS BLOCKING MY VIEW! HONK HONK HONK!!

ALL MINIVANS, TRUCKS AND BUSES TO THE LEFT! AACK! YOU CUT ME OFF! DON'T YOU SEE ME DOWN HERE?? AACK!
HONK

THE DYING BREED OF SPORTS CAR OWNERS... SO COOL, YET SO INVISIBLE...
Guisewite

FILTHY WINDOWS. DINGED DOORS. GRUNGY WHEELS. DINGY CHROME.
WASH ME

STICKY STEERING WHEEL. DISGUSTING SEATS. GROSS CARPETS. ROTTING TRASH BAGS. SMEARED DIALS.
WASH

Click.
WASH

MY CAR EITHER HAS A DEAD BATTERY OR IS JUST TOO EMBARRASSED TO GO ANYWHERE.
Guisewite

I CAN'T SHOP FOR A NEW CAR UNTIL I KNOW WHAT I CAN AFFORD...WON'T KNOW WHAT I CAN AFFORD UNTIL I KNOW WHAT MY CURRENT CAR'S WORTH...

...CAN'T FIGURE OUT WHAT MY CURRENT CAR'S WORTH UNTIL I TAKE IT TO A DEALER... ...CAN'T TAKE IT TO A DEALER UNTIL IT GETS FIXED...
diet

...CAN'T GET IT FIXED UNTIL IT GETS TOWED...CAN'T GET IT TOWED UNTIL I FIND MY AAA CARD... CAN'T FIND MY AAA CARD UNTIL I CLEAN MY PURSE.....

RATS. BACK TO THE HANDBAG.
Guisewite

SHALL I TOW YOUR CAR TO THE CROOK WHO SOLD YOU YOUR LAST BATTERY, OR THE SWINDLER WHO PUT IN YOUR NEW STARTER...
TOW

...THE RIP-OFF ARTIST WHO INSTALLED THE CORRODED FUEL PUMP, OR THE THIEF WHO MONKEYED WITH YOUR CARBURETOR...
TOW

...OR SHALL I JUST HAUL IT TO THE USED CAR LOT SO YOU CAN SELL IT AS IS ?
TOW

THE USED CAR LOT? DON'T BE RIDICULOUS! I MIGHT BE TAKEN ADVANTAGE OF!
TOW
Guisewite

YOU CAN'T SIMPLY GO BUY A CAR, CATHY! YOU HAVE TO SEE ALL THE CARS! TEST DRIVE THEM! TRY THEM ON! COMPARE! GO BACK! COMPARE SOME MORE!

STUDY CONSUMER REPORTS! PORE OVER THE BLUE BOOK! TALK ON THE INTERNET! RESEARCH OPTION PACKAGES! RESEARCH LEASES! RESEARCH WARRANTIES! RESEARCH CRASH TESTS! RESEARCH RESALE VALUES!

CALCULATE REBATES, MAP OUT A NEGOTIATION STRATEGY... AND THEN GO BUY A CAR!!

WHERE'S THIS ENERGY WHEN WE WANT A MAN TO GO IN A MALL??
A MALL?? BLEAH! THAT'S SHOPPING!
Guisewite

1970's
I WANT A CAR THAT'S OPEN, FREE AND, LIKE, COMPLETELY INDIVIDUALISTIC!
CARS

1980's
I WANT A CAR THAT'S A HOT, SEXY SYMBOL OF MY PERSONAL POWER AND INDEPENDENCE!
CARS

1990's
JUST POINT ME TO SOMETHING CHEAP AND INOFFENSIVE AND MAKE SURE IT WILL LAST A LONG TIME BECAUSE I NEVER WANT TO GO THROUGH THIS REPULSIVE PROCESS AGAIN!
Guisewite

THE AMERICAN CAR BUYER: FROM LOVE AFFAIR TO ARRANGED MARRIAGE.
ALSO, STICK IN AN ALARM SO NO ONE ELSE WILL RUN OFF WITH IT.

OH, SURE, SHE HAS PERFECT THIGHS... SHE PROBABLY SPENDS THREE HOURS A DAY ON THE STAIR MACHINE!
SWIMWEAR

OF **COURSE** SHE HAS A CUTE REAR AND A FLAT LITTLE STOMACH...SHE PROBABLY GOES TO THE GYM FIVE NIGHTS A WEEK AND SPENDS HALF THE WEEKEND WITH A PERSONAL TRAINER!

HAH! SOME OF US HAVE BETTER THINGS TO DO WITH OUR TIME!!

EAT, FOR INSTANCE.
FOOD COURT
Guisewite

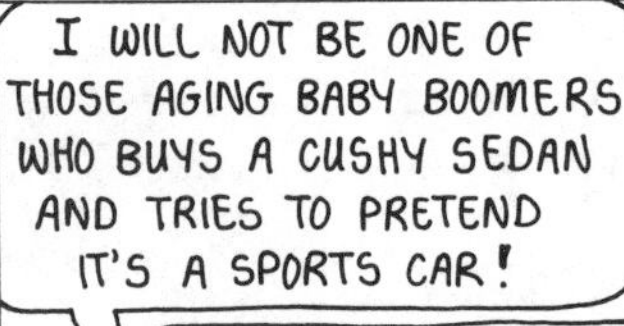
I WILL NOT BE ONE OF THOSE AGING BABY BOOMERS WHO BUYS A CUSHY SEDAN AND TRIES TO PRETEND IT'S A SPORTS CAR!

OF COURSE YOU WON'T.
SPORT SEDANS

I REFUSE TO EMBRACE PUSH BUTTONS AND GIANT DIGITAL DISPLAYS AS "HIGH TECH," INSTEAD OF THE BLATANT ADMISSION OF LAZINESS AND BLINDNESS THAT THEY ARE!

OF COURSE YOU DO.
SPORT SEDANS

LET MY GENERATION CRUISE-CONTROL INTO OLD AGE! I REFUSE TO GIVE IN TO......

...OH, MY... THIS DOES FEEL GOOD...
TO REAWAKEN THE REBEL, THERE'S ROOM FOR A TRIPLE ESPRESSO IN THE CUP HOLDER.

IF I BUY THE SENSIBLE FOUR-DOOR WITH ROOM FOR KIDS, AM I OPENING THE COSMIC DOOR TO **HAVING** CHILDREN... OR WILL ALL PROSPECTIVE MEN IGNORE ME BECAUSE I LOOK AS THOUGH I'M ALREADY A MOTHER?

IF I BUY THE SPORTY TWO-DOOR THAT SCREAMS "SINGLE AND CHILDLESS", DO I LOOK AVAILABLE, OR DO I JUST LOOK DESPERATE?

DO I PRESENT MYSELF AS A FULLY EQUIPPED MOTHERHOOD PACKAGE... OR AS A CAREFREE SINGLE GAL? WHICH WILL MY POTENTIAL MATE RESPOND TO?? WHAT WILL APPEAL TO HIM?? WHAT'S HE LOOKING FOR??

SHE'S BACK, AND THIS TIME SHE'S BROUGHT HER HYPOTHETICAL HUSBAND.
FINANCING
SALES MANAGER

WHEW! WHAT A RIDE! WHAT DID YOU THINK??
IT FELT EXACTLY LIKE THE NINE OTHER CARS I TEST DROVE THIS WEEK.

NO, HA, HA! I MEAN THE MULTI-LINK INDEPENDENT SUSPENSION! THE PRECISION CORNERING!
IT FELT EXACTLY LIKE ALL THE OTHER CARS.

YOU **HAD** TO NOTICE THE 24-VALVE, HIGH-OUTPUT V6 ENGINE... THE 4-WHEEL ANTI-LOCK BRAKES... THE REDUCED DRAG COEFFICIENT...

ALL CARS FEEL THE SAME. THEY EVEN LOOK THE SAME TO ME.

AAGH!!
THIS MUST BE HOW A MAN FEELS WHEN A WOMAN TAKES HIM SHOE SHOPPING...

WE'RE NOT SUPPOSED TO HAGGLE, BUT I THINK I COULD KNOCK $400 OFF THE PRICE IF YOU COMMIT TODAY!
I'M NOT INTERESTED.
NEW

MY BOSS WILL KILL ME, BUT I'M GOING TO THROW IN THE OPTIONAL ALLOY WHEELS!
I'M NOT INTERESTED.
FINANCING

I'LL KICK BACK HALF OF MY COMMISSION!!
I'M NOT INTERESTED.

SURROUNDED BY CARS SHE HATES AND SALESPEOPLE SHE CAN'T STAND, A WOMAN REACHES HER PINNACLE OF DESIRABILITY.
TELL ME WHAT YOU WANT!
TELL ME WHAT YOU NEED!
WHAT WILL MAKE YOU HAPPY?!
Guisewite

FOR THE RUGGED INDIVIDUALIST IN ALL OF US... THE SPORT UTILITY VEHICLE!!

OF COURSE, IT HAS A CUSHIONED SUSPENSION SO YOU WON'T FEEL ANY BUMPS... A SOUNDPROOF CABIN SO YOU WON'T HEAR ANY ANNOYING BIRD NOISES... CLIMATE CONTROL ZONES AND HEATED SEATS SO YOU WON'T GET CHILLY...

GIANT WIPERS SO YOU WON'T HAVE TO LOOK AT ANY BUGS ...AND ELECTRONIC BUTTONS SO YOU WON'T STRAIN ANY FINGERS ADJUSTING THE MIRRORS ....AT LAST, YOU CAN BE ONE WITH NATURE!

...UNLESS YOU GET A FLAT TIRE, IN WHICH CASE A FLEET OF ROADSIDE ASSISTANCE VANS WILL RUSH TO YOUR SIDE SO YOU WON'T GET ANY DIRT ON YOUR HIKING BOOTS.
Guisewite

IMAGINE YOURSELF ROARING AWAY FROM THE STRESS OF THE CITY!
SPORT UTILITY VEHICLES

IMAGINE YOURSELF TOSSING A CANOE ON TOP AND HEADING FOR THE MOUNTAINS!

IMAGINE MYSELF HAULING FIFTEEN BAGS OF CLOTHING BACK TO THE MALL SO I COULD MAKE THE FIRST MONTH'S PAYMENT.

PERFECT! SHE COMES STANDARD WITH 90 CUBIC FEET OF CARGO SPACE AND AN OPTIONAL TRAILER HITCH!
Guisewite

THE $50,000 LUXURY PERFORMANCE SEDAN! GRAND SYMBOL OF OUR TIMES!
LUXURY SEDAN

IT SAYS, "I'VE ACHIEVED!" "I'VE SUCCEEDED!" "I'VE MADE IT!" "I STRIVE, THEREFORE I AM!!"

...OR MAYBE SOMETHING EVEN MORE POIGNANTLY PERSONAL...

"I'M BROKE, THEREFORE I LEASE."
DOES THIS COUNTRY KNOW HOW TO KEEP UP APPEARANCES, OR WHAT??
Guisewite

WHAT ON EARTH ARE YOU DOING LOOKING AT $20,000 CARS, CATHY?!

THAT'S WHAT NEW CARS COST, MOM. A BASIC CAR WITH THE BASIC STUFF IS $20,000!
DON'T BE RIDICULOUS! THAT'S MORE THAN OUR FIRST HOUSE COST!

MOTHER, WAKE UP! GYM SHOES COST $100! PANTYHOSE COST $9! LIPSTICK COSTS $15! CARS COST $20,000, AND IF YOU OWN ONE, IT COSTS MORE TO PARK IT AT THE RESTAURANT THAN IT USED TO COST TO EAT DINNER!

TWO ICED TEAS: $5.50.
I EITHER NEED TO GET OUT MORE OR LOCK MYSELF IN THE HOUSE ONCE AND FOR ALL AND BE DONE WITH IT.
Guisewite

WE'RE WILLING TO GIVE YOU A $2,800 TRADE-IN ON YOUR CAR, CATHY!
$2,800?? ARE YOU JOKING?? ARE YOU OUT OF YOUR MIND??!!
ALES

HOW GULLIBLE DO I LOOK?? HOW UNINFORMED DO YOU THINK I AM?? DO YOU THINK I HAVEN'T DONE MY RESEARCH?? DO YOU THINK I DIDN'T STUDY THE CHARTS? $2,800?? HAH! HAH!!

FEEL FREE TO ADVERTISE ON YOUR OWN AND SPEND THE NEXT SIX WEEKENDS CAMPED BY THE PHONE.
ALES
Guisewite

$2,800 IT IS.
ANOTHER "CONSUMER REPORTS" AFICIONADO STRUCK DOWN BY THE CHEAP THRILL OF INSTANT GRATIFICATION.

SIMPLY ADD THE CAPITALIZATION COST REDUCTION PLUS SALES TAX AND INTEREST LOST ON THE CAP COST REDUCTION... SUBTRACT INCOME TAX SAVINGS ON INTEREST LOST... ADD MONTHLY PAYMENTS, TAX, ACQUISITION FEE, DISPOSITION FEE, WEAR AND TEAR FEE, ADMINISTRATION FEE, EXCESS MILEAGE FEE, EXTENDED WARRANTY FEE AND GAP PROTECTION FEE...
LEASE

...CALCULATE THE RESIDUAL VALUE AGAINST THE HIGHER DOWN, HIGHER MONTHLY PAYMENTS AND INTEREST LOST WHEN **BUYING** A CAR... AND YOU'LL SEE WHY 30% OF ALL NEW CARS ARE NOW LEASED!

YOU'VE GIVEN ME A HEADACHE. I WANT TO GO HOME.
BINGO! SIGN HERE AND YOU WON'T HAVE TO THINK ABOUT IT FOR ANOTHER THREE YEARS.
NEW CAR LEASES

IF THIS COUNTRY'S GOING DOWN THE DRAIN, IT'S BECAUSE NOBODY OWNS ANYTHING ANYMORE!

EVERYONE MAKES PAYMENTS ON EVERYTHING, BUT NO ONE ACTUALLY OWNS ANYTHING!

WITHOUT OWNERSHIP, THERE'S NO RESPONSIBILITY... WITHOUT RESPONSIBILITY, NO COMMITMENT... WITHOUT COMMITMENT, NO ROOTS... WITHOUT ROOTS, NO TREES... NO FORESTS... NO EARTH... NO PEOPLE... **AND WITH NO PEOPLE AND NO EARTH, WHAT'S THE POINT OF HAVING SOME OVERPRICED NEW CAR IN THE GARAGE??!**

MY MOM: A TOUGH SELL, BUT AN IMPOSSIBLE LEASE.
DOES ANYONE HAVE AN ASPIRIN I CAN BORROW?!
NEW CAR LEASE
LOW DOWN FAB TERMS

I HAVE BROCHURES ON 42 CARS, MINIVANS AND SPORT UTILITY VEHICLES... COMPARISON SURVEYS FROM 25 MAGAZINES... 17 ARTICLES DOWNLOADED FROM FOUR ON-LINE SERVICES...

...98 OPINIONS ON THE BRILLIANCE OR IDIOCY OF LEASING VERSUS BUYING, INCLUDING DOCUMENTATION ON THE RAMIFICATIONS ON INSURANCE, WARRANTIES AND TAXES.

IN THREE WEEKS, I'VE COLLECTED 6,000 NEW PIECES OF KNOWLEDGE, AND AM FURTHER FROM OWNING SOMETHING TO DRIVE THAN WHEN I BEGAN!

I'M ON THE INFORMATION SUPERHIGHWAY, HOWEVER I'M GOING BACKWARD, AND I'M SITTING ON A BUS.
BUS #276 ZONE 7

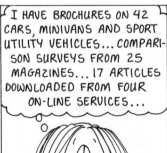

WE'VE AGREED ON THE CAR, PRICE AND TERMS. WHY AREN'T YOU SIGNING, CATHY ?
I'M AFRAID AS SOON AS I SIGN, YOU'LL RUN TO THE SALES OFFICE AND HAVE A LITTLE PARTY.

DON'T BE SILLY. THE SALES OFFICE IS WAY TOO SMALL FOR A PARTY! AS SOON AS YOU SIGN, WE'RE CLOSING DOWN THE WHOLE DEALERSHIP AND HEADING TO A BANQUET HALL FOR A FULL CATERED EVENT!

LITTLE PARTY?? HOO, BOY, NO! WE'LL BE LAUGHING AND SHRIEKING ABOUT THE DEAL WE GOT YOU TO SIGN FOR MONTHS TO COME! HA, HA!

OH, VERY FUNNY! HA, HA! OK. I'LL SIGN.
THE SALESPERSON'S ULTIMATE NEGOTIATING TOOL: THE TRUTH.
Guisewite

DON'T CRASH THE NEW CAR ON THE WAY HOME FROM THE DEALER! DON'T CRASH THE NEW CAR ON THE WAY HOME FROM THE DEALER!

IT WOULD BE SO HUMILIATING! WHAT WOULD I SAY? I COULDN'T TELL MY FRIENDS! I COULDN'T FACE THE DEALER! HOW COULD I EVEN ADMIT IT TO THE INSURANCE COMPANY??

I'D HAVE TO SNEAK OUT OF TOWN IN SHAME! AACK! JUST GET THE NEW CAR HOME WITHOUT CRASHING! GET THE CAR HOME WITHOUT CRASHING!

OK. I'M READY FOR THE KEYS NOW.
A RECORD! FROM ZERO TO 60 ANXIETIES IN TEN SECONDS!
SHOWROO
CLICK!
Guisewite

I BOUGHT A CAR TODAY, MOM.
YOU BOUGHT A CAR, CATHY??

I GOT SICK OF LOOKING AT BODIES. SICK OF HEARING ABOUT POWER AND DRIVE. SICK OF TRYING TO FIND PERFECT COMPATIBILITY.

I JUST PICKED ONE. JUST SHUT MY EYES AND PICKED ONE AND I'LL LIVE WITH IT AS LONG AS HUMANLY POSSIBLE!

QUICK! ROUND UP THE MEN!! SHE'S IN THE COMMITMENT MODE!!
Guisewite

LEOTARD WITH MATCHING TIGHTS, WRISTBANDS AND SCRUNCHY... NO. LOOKS LIKE I'M TRYING TO LOOK TOO GOOD.
BAGGY SWEATSUIT... NO. LOOKS LIKE I'M TRYING TO NOT LOOK TOO GOOD...
SHORTS AND TANK TOP... ...NO. LOOKS LIKE I'M TRYING TO LOOK LIKE I'M NOT TRYING TO LOOK LIKE I'M TRYING TO LOOK GOOD...
ONCE AGAIN, I'VE EXHAUSTED MYSELF WITHOUT EVER LEAVING THE LOCKER ROOM.
Guisewite

QUIT NOW, **MOM**!! QUIT WHILE YOU CAN! THE CON-VERSATION IS DOOMED! GET OUT WHILE THERE'S A CHANCE FOR MUTUAL DIGNITY!!

SURE, CATHY. SIMON AND I WOULD LOVE TO GO OUT! WHO ARE YOU BRINGING?
ME! I'M BRINGING ME!
CLEAN UP YOUR OWN MESS

MY CHARM
MY WIT
MY COMPASSION
MY CONVERSATION
MY COMPANY
MY INSIGHTS
MY ENERGY
MY PERSPECTIVE
MY INTERESTS
MY OPINIONS AND
MY SENSE OF HUMOR!

BUT WHAT **PERSON** ARE YOU BRINGING?

HOW GREAT MUST A SOLO ACT GET BEFORE IT HAS THE APPEAL OF A MEDIOCRE DUET?...
CATHY

HOW ARE YOU GETTING DRESSED FOR TONIGHT, CHARLENE?
OH, I DON'T KNOW... PROBABLY JUST JEANS.

NO. NOT **WHAT** ARE YOU WEARING... HOW ARE YOU **GETTING DRESSED?** HOW DO YOU TRY ON ALL THE COMBINATIONS WHEN YOU'RE MARRIED?? WHERE DO YOU HIDE THE PILES OF REJECTS??

DO YOU OBSESS RIGHT THERE IN FRONT OF YOUR HUSBAND, OR DO YOU LOCK HIM OUT OF THE ROOM?? WHAT IF HE WALKS IN WHEN YOU HAVE SIX PAIRS OF SHOES OUT?? WHAT DO YOU DO ABOUT THE PRICE TAGS?? HOW DOES IT ALL HAPPEN?? HOW DOES IT WORK????

WHEN YOU'RE SINGLE, GETTING DRESSED IS AN ACHIEVEMENT. WHEN YOU'RE MARRIED, IT MUST BE A MIRACLE.

WE'LL TAKE OUR CAR BECAUSE WE'RE THE MARRIED PEOPLE.

SIMON WILL DRIVE BECAUSE HE'S THE HUSBAND, AND I'LL SIT IN FRONT NEXT TO HIM BECAUSE WE'RE THE COUPLE.

EVERYTHING OK BACK THERE?

SINGLENESS AT ITS WEIRDEST: FROM DOUBLE DATE TO DATE AND A HALF.

WILL YOU BE NEEDING THIS CHAIR?
NO. NO ONE ELSE IS COMING. THE FOURTH CHAIR IS NOT NEEDED.

IS THIS AN EXTRA NAPKIN?
YES. TAKE THE NAPKIN! TAKE THE SILVERWARE! TAKE THE GLASS! TAKE THE BREAD PLATE! TAKE ONE FOURTH OF THE SUGAR PACKS!

CLEAR OUT THE ACCOUTERMENTS! ELIMINATE THE SPACE! REMOVE A QUARTER OF THE OXYGEN IF YOU WANT! I'M ALONE! NO ONE IS JOINING ME!!

...SO, DO YOU GUYS KNOW ANYONE??
UM, GEE... WHEW! WE'LL HAVE TO THINK ABOUT IT....
GUISEWITE

UM...DID YOU WANT TO COME IN FOR COFFEE?
YAWN HO, HUM...NO... LOOK AT THE TIME...

WELL...UM... MAYBE WE'LL HAVE DINNER AGAIN SOMETIME...
SURE... UM...WE'LL GIVE YOU A CALL.

WELL, I'M PRETTY BUSY FOR THE NEXT FEW WEEKS, BUT IT WAS GREAT...REALLY!
OH, YES! A GREAT EVENING! TALK TO YOU SOON!

HAVING HAD MORE RECENT EXPERIENCE, ONLY THE SINGLE WOMAN KNOWS FOR SURE THAT A DUMP HAS JUST OCCURRED.
WHEW!
GUISEWITE

REBECCA
I OWN A DEMURE, TAILORED NEW PANTSUIT. LOOK AT ME!

SUZANNE
I OWN A SMART, SOPHISTICATED NEW DRESS. LOOK AT ME!

MAUREEN
I OWN AN IMPECCABLY CHIC NEW SUIT. LOOK AT ME!

CATHY
I OWN A FIVE-YEAR LOAN ON A NEW CAR. LOOK AT ME THROUGH THE WINDSHIELD!
$
GUISEWITE

I BOUGHT A NEW CAR THIS YEAR AND, THEREFORE, WILL NOT BE BUYING ANY NEW FALL CLOTHES, CHARLENE!
RECEPTIONIST

I HAVE A HUGE NEW FINANCIAL OBLIGATION, AND PAYING IT OFF IS MY UTMOST AND ONLY CONCERN. NOTHING WILL DERAIL ME FROM MY COURSE OF FRUGAL RESPONSIBILITY!

LOOK AT MY NEW SHOES.
NEW SHOES?
RECEPTIONIST

LIKE A POWER SURGE WIPING OUT A COMPUTER, THE SMELL OF FRESH LEATHER SHORT-CIRCUITS ANOTHER WOMAN'S BRAIN.
RECEPTIONIST
Guisewite

THE CLASSIC NAVY SKIRT. BOUGHT IN 1983. SHORTENED TO A MINI IN 1994.

THE CLASSIC TWEED SKIRT. BOUGHT IN 1978. SHORTENED TO A MINI IN 1994.

THE CLASSIC CAMEL SKIRT. BOUGHT IN 1986. SHORTENED TO A MINI IN 1994.

SIX PERFECT SKIRTS, UNWORN FOR YEARS, IRREVOCABLY CHOPPED OFF A FEW MONTHS BEFORE EVERY NEW SKIRT IN THE COUNTRY WOULD LOOK EXACTLY THE WAY THEY USED TO.

FALL, 1995: WOMEN'S RETAIL FINALLY GETS ITS WISH.
RUN FOR YOUR LIFE! THE CUSTOMERS ARE BACK!
KNEE LENGTH SKIRTS
LONG
Guisewite

THE NEW JACKET IS WORN BUTTONED, WHICH OBLITERATES ANY SIGN OF A CHEST, AND IS CROPPED TO FALL EXACTLY ON THE WIDEST PART OF THE HIP.

IT'S WORN WITH A KNEE-GRAZING SKIRT AND MODEST PUMPS, THE COMBINATION OF WHICH MAKES THE THIGHS LOOK MAMMOTH AND THE CALVES LOOK SQUATTY.

ACCESSORIES ARE NONEXISTENT, EXCEPT FOR A TEENY MOLDED PURSE, TOO SMALL TO HOLD ANYTHING BUT THE HANKIE YOU'LL BE WEEPING INTO WHEN YOU GET A LOAD OF YOURSELF IN A FULL-LENGTH MIRROR.

WAAH!
AT LAST. FASHION LIVES UP TO ITS PROMISE!
Guisewite

THE CONSUMER HAS SPOKEN, AND THE FASHION INDUSTRY HAS FINALLY LISTENED! NO MORE GIMMICKS! NO MORE GOOFY TRENDS!
FALL FASHION

WE'VE CONSIDERED EVERY BODY TYPE, STUDIED EVERY LIFESTYLE, SCRUTINIZED EVERY ASPECT OF A WOMAN'S WARDROBE NEEDS...

...AND HAVE FILLED OUR STORES WITH THE CLASSIC, TASTEFUL, GO ANYWHERE, DO ANYTHING, ABSOLUTELY ESSENTIAL GARMENT FOR FALL: **THE SLEEVELESS SHIFT!!**
SLEEVELESS SHIFTS
SLEEVELESS SHIFTS
SLEEVE-LESS SHIFTS

IT'S 40° OUT. MY ARMS WILL FREEZE.
OOPS.
THE CUSTOMERS ARE ALWAYS ONE STEP AHEAD OF US...
SLEEVELESS SHIFTS
SLEEVELESS SHIFTS
SLEEVE-LESS SHIFTS
Guisewite

FASHION IN THE '90s! WE'RE BORROWING FITTED JACKETS AND PENCIL SKIRTS FROM THE '40s...

WE'RE BORROWING PRIM ACCESSORIES AND MODEST PUMPS FROM THE '50s...

WE'RE BORROWING DEMURE SHIFTS AND TWINSETS FROM THE '60s...WE'RE BORROWING MENSWEAR FABRICS FROM THE '70s....

AND WE'RE BORROWING FROM FIVE CREDIT CARD COMPANIES TO PAY FOR IT.
I LOVE A DECADE WITH A THEME!
GUISEWITE

FADS ARE GONE! TRENDS ARE GONE! CLASSIC ELEGANCE IS HERE TO STAY!
HOW LONG THIS TIME?
Classic Elegance

IT WAS GRUNGE ONE SEASON, BABY DOLL DRESSES THE NEXT... GRANNY GOWNS ONE SEASON, RUBBER CAT SUITS THE NEXT... PLATFORM FLATS ONE SEASON, STRAPPY STILETTOS THE NEXT...
Classic Elegance

HOW LONG WILL CLASSIC ELEGANCE BE IN?? UNTIL MY NEXT CHARGE CARD STATEMENT COMES??

RETAIL HAS FINALLY SHOT ITSELF IN THE FOOT.
FORTUNATELY, WE'RE WEARING OUR ANKLE-HIGH, CHUNKY-HEELED, WAFFLE-BOTTOMED JODHPUR BOOTS.
Guisewite

I'VE LOST WEIGHT!
...BUT MY SKIRT IS TOO TIGHT.

...BUT I'VE LOST WEIGHT!
...BUT MY PANTS ARE TOO TIGHT!

...BUT I'VE LOST WEIGHT!
...BUT MY DRESS IS TOO TIGHT!

FALL FASHION'S NEW ATTITUDE: CONFIDENCE, CONFIDENCE, CONFIDENCE!
I'VE LOST WEIGHT, I TELL YOU! I'VE LOST WEIGHT!
RECEPTION

IF I WERE 15 POUNDS THINNER AND 7 INCHES TALLER, I COULD SEE HOW THIS SUIT COULD BE FABULOUS.

IF I HAD AN EVENT TO ATTEND WHERE I COULD SIT IN MOODY LIGHTING ON A SLIGHTLY RAISED PLATFORM THAT WOULD DISTORT MY HIP-TO-BUST PROPORTION, I COULD SEE WHERE THIS COULD LOOK INCREDIBLE.

IF I COULD SIMULTANEOUSLY RE-CREATE MY GOOD HAIR DAY OF 1979, MY GOOD FACE DAY OF 1992 AND THE 15 MINUTES OF COMPLETE INNER CONFIDENCE I EXPERIENCED IN 1985, I COULD SEE THAT THIS OUTFIT WOULD BE PERFECT.

WILL YOU PUT IT ON HOLD FOR A COUPLE OF HOURS?
GOD BLESS THE FEMALE SPIRIT.
Guisewite

IMAGINE A PARTY!
THE LAST PARTY I WENT TO, THE HOSTESS WORE CUT-OFFS AND FLIP-FLOPS.

IMAGINE A DATE!
MY LAST DATE PICKED ME UP IN BLUE JEANS AND A T-SHIRT.

IMAGINE TRAVEL!
ON MY LAST TRIP, THE MOST DRESSED-UP PERSON ON THE PLANE WORE SWEATS AND A MATCHING HAIR SCRUNCHY.

IMAGINE STANDING IN YOUR BATHROOM THINKING HOW FABULOUS YOU LOOK.
SOLD!

WE MAY DRESS FOR OTHERS, BUT WE DREAM ALONE.
Guisewite

THE FAUX ZEBRA JACKET... THE FAUX LEOPARD SKIRT... THE FAUX GIRAFFE SCARF... THE FAUX TORTOISE GLASSES...

THE FAUX TIGER GLOVES... THE FAUX CROC BAG... THE FAUX CHEETAH BOOTS... THE FAUX BEAR COAT...

PUT IT ALL TOGETHER AND WHAT DO YOU HAVE??

THE FAUX PAS.
Guisewite

WHAT ARE YOU DOING FOR LUNCH, CATHY?
I HAVE TO GO UPDATE MY LIP.
RECEPTIONIST

WHAT??
THIS FALL'S MORE DEMURE STYLES CALL FOR A MORE SUBTLE LIP.

THE DEEPLY HUED, POWER-FULLY SEDUCTIVE, HIGH-GLOSS LIP IS STILL IN FOR EVENING... ...BUT FOR DAY, THE MORE PASTEL, GENTEEL LIP IS RE-QUIRED. I NEED TO GO FIND MY NEW LIP FOR THE....
FALL FASHION

AAGH!!
WHY DO THEY ASK WHEN THEY NEVER WANT TO KNOW?
RECEPTIO
GUISEWITE

THIS YEAR, THE SMALL SHOE IS BIG!
THE SMALL SHOE IS BIG?
FALL '95

THE SMALL SHOE IS BIG! THE SMALL BELT IS BIG! THE SMALL BAG IS BIG! THE SMALL HIP IS BIG! THE SMALL SHOULDER IS BIG! THE SMALL WAIST IS BIG! THE SMALL THIGH IS BIG!

EVERYTHING THAT'S SMALL IS BIG EXCEPT CHESTS AND HAIR! BIG CHESTS ARE STILL BIG, AND BIG HAIR IS HUGE!!
FALL '95

AS USUAL, MY TWO QUALIFYING FEATURES HAVE BEEN ELIMINATED FROM THE RUNNING.
GUISEWITE

6:30 AM: I'M UP!

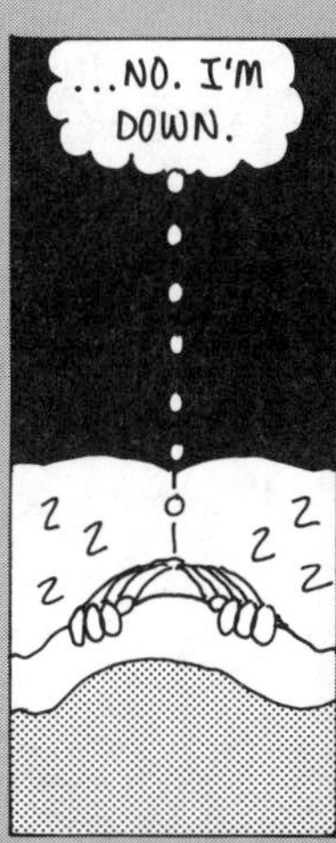
...NO. I'M DOWN.

7:00 AM: I'M UP!

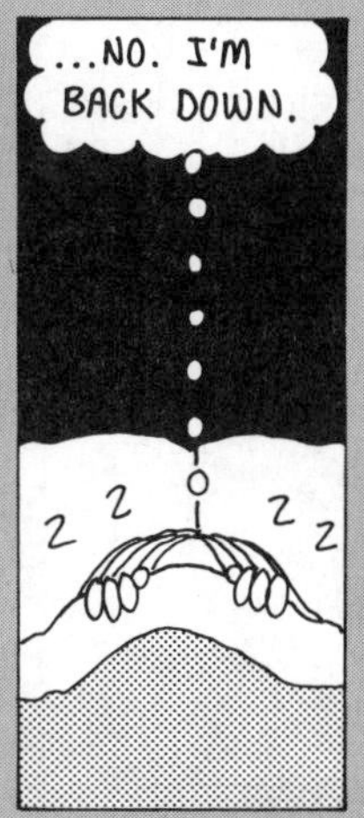
...NO. I'M BACK DOWN.

7:15 AM: I'M UP! DEFI-NITELY UP! ...NO. I'M DOWN. ...NO. I'M UP! ...NO. DOWN. ...NO! UP! ...NO. DOWN...

ALTHOUGH SHE WORKS ON IT FOR AN HOUR EACH MORNING, DOING 25 REPS EACH TIME, ANOTHER WOMAN IS STILL VAGUELY SURPRISED TO FIND THE ONLY TONED AREA OF HER BODY IS THE PROCRASTINATION MUSCLE.
GUISEWITE

"$65"?? "DRY CLEAN ONLY"?? THIS IS A WHITE T-SHIRT!!
YOU'LL WEAR IT ALL WEEK!
TEES

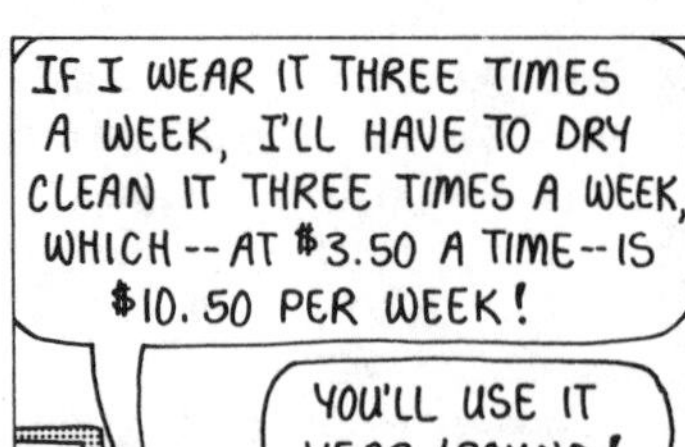
IF I WEAR IT THREE TIMES A WEEK, I'LL HAVE TO DRY CLEAN IT THREE TIMES A WEEK, WHICH -- AT $3.50 A TIME -- IS $10.50 PER WEEK!

YOU'LL USE IT YEAR 'ROUND!

IF I USE IT YEAR 'ROUND AT $10.50 PER WEEK, THAT'S $546 JUST FOR CLEANING!
A WARDROBE STAPLE! ...SEE?? IT'S SO MUCH MORE THAN A $65 WHITE T-SHIRT!

IT'S A $611 WHITE T-SHIRT!
OR ONLY $305.50 IF YOU BUY TWO AND ROTATE.
Guisewite

FALL DRESSING: THE MAGAZINE
SLEEK SOPHISTICATION

FALL DRESSING: THE COMMERCIAL
POLISHED REFINEMENT

FALL DRESSING: THE STORE
UNDERSTATED GLAMOUR

FALL DRESSING: THE HOME
WHERE'S A STAPLER?? MY SKIRT HEM TORE! WHERE'S A BLOUSE?? ANY CLEAN BLOUSE!! WHERE ARE SCISSORS SO I CAN CUT ONE GOOD LEG FROM TWO PAIRS OF PANTYHOSE??!
Guisewite

HOW COULD I HAVE SPENT ALL THAT MONEY ON A NEW CAR?? WHAT WAS I THINKING???

...AND NOW NEW CLOTHES. NEW CLOTHES IN THE TRUNK OF THE NEW CAR! I'M DISGUSTED WITH MYSELF! I'M SICK! I'M ILL!!
Mall

I AM NEVER SPENDING ANOTHER PENNY AGAIN! A NEW REGIME HAS BEGUN! FROM THIS DAY FORWARD, I VOW TO LIVE A FRUGAL, MODEST AND THRIFTY LIFE!!
GIFTS
GIFTS
Mall

ANOTHER WOMAN HITS THE BOTTOM OF THE BARREL ONLY TO FIND IT LINED WITH CHRISTMAS CATALOGS.
GIFTS
Guisewite

. . . . OK, MOM . . . . . . OK, MOM . . . . . OK, MOM . . .

. . . . OK, MOM . . . . OK, MOM . . . . YOU'RE RIGHT, MOM . . . . OK, MOM . . . . BYE, MOM . . . . .

COOKIES

SOME PEOPLE HAVE TO GET THE LAST WORD IN. I HAVE TO GET THE LAST COOKIE IN.

THE CHILDREN WERE IMPOSSIBLE THIS MORNING!

THEY WOULDN'T LISTEN! THEY WOULDN'T DO ANYTHING I ASKED! THEY TURNED THE TEENSIEST DISAGREEMENT INTO A HUGE PRODUCTION!!

THEY HURLED ME ON AN EMOTIONAL ROLLER COASTER AND DROVE ME RIGHT TO THE BRINK OF INSANITY!!

...sigh... I CAN'T WAIT TO SEE THEM AGAIN....
WHO KNEW THAT PARENTING WOULD BE SO MUCH LIKE DATING?

IN BUSINESS I HAVE TO BE THE TOUGH ONE OR NO ONE WILL TAKE ME SERIOUSLY...

WITH MY CHILDREN I HAVE TO BE THE TOUGH ONE BECAUSE NO ONE ELSE WILL MAKE OR ENFORCE ANY RULES...

HAVING ACHIEVED THE DREAM OF DOING, BEING AND HAVING IT ALL, THE '90s WOMAN STRIVES FOR AN EVEN LOFTIER GOAL...

I WANT TO GET TO BE THE WIMP FOR A FEW MINUTES!!
NOT NOW, ANDREA. YOU HAVE A CLIENT ON LINE ONE AND A SON WHO REFUSES TO TAKE A NAP ON LINE TWO.

WORK WORK WORK WORK

BUY GROCERIES
GET GAS
GET CASH
PICK UP CLEANING
DROP OFF VIDEOS

MAMA!!

...SO MUCH FOR MY TEN MINUTES OF SELF-PAMPERING TRANSITION TIME....
IT'S NOT ALL LOST. YOU'RE SITTING IN A PUDDLE OF BUBBLE BATH YOUR SON DUMPED ON THE FLOOR.

HI, ANDREA. WAIT'LL YOU HEAR WHAT...
I CAN'T TALK, CATHY. I'M PUTTING THE KIDS TO BED.

IT'LL ONLY TAKE A MINUTE.
I DON'T HAVE A MINUTE. I HAVE A 35-SECOND WINDOW OF TIME BEFORE "JUST TIRED ENOUGH" KICKS INTO "OVER-TIRED AND IMPOSSIBLE".

I JUST HAVE TO TELL YOU THE FUNNIEST THING THAT...
AAGH! TOO LATE!! I SPENT AN HOUR GETTING THEM IN THE MOOD FOR BED AND NOW IT'S OVER! NOW THEY'LL NEVER GO TO SLEEP AND IT'S ALL YOUR FAULT!!

WHY DON'T WE USE THE ANSWERING MACHINE, ANDREA?
I SWORE I WOULDN'T BE ONE OF THOSE MOTHERS WHO NEGLECTS HER FRIENDS.

YOU JUST TOLD GUS HE COULDN'T HAVE A COOKIE! HOW COULD YOU BREAK DOWN AND GIVE HIM COOKIES??

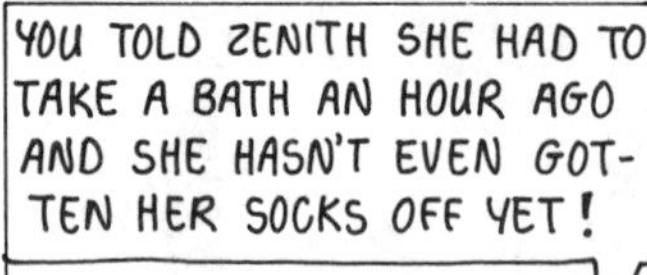
YOU TOLD ZENITH SHE HAD TO TAKE A BATH AN HOUR AGO AND SHE HASN'T EVEN GOTTEN HER SOCKS OFF YET!

YOU TOLD THEM ABSOLUTELY NO VIDEOS UNTIL THEY CLEANED UP... AND THEY'RE PLOPPED IN THE MIDDLE OF THE MESS WATCHING VIDEOS!

THE IMPORTANT THING IS, WE'RE BEING CONSISTENT.
SHOULD WE MENTION BEDTIME, OR SHOULD WE MAINTAIN SOME DIGNITY AND JUST LET THEM STAY UP?

I CAN DO IT!
I CAN MAKE IT HAPPEN!
I CAN SUCCEED!
I HAVE WHAT IT TAKES!! I AM UNSTOPPABLE!!
I FINALLY GOT CONNECTED TO MY PERSONAL POWER, AND IT HUNG UP ON ME.
WHY DO HUMANS GET SO WORKED UP TO WATCH TV?...
CLICK.
GUISEWITE

A SINGLE WOMAN, FIVE MINUTES AND A BATHROOM:
squirt

A WORKING MOTHER, FIVE MINUTES AND A BATHROOM:
BAM BAM
HONEY?
MOM!
MA MA
BAM BAM
FIVE MINUTES! PLEASE! JUST LET ME HAVE FIVE MINUTES TO WRITE THANK-YOU NOTES FROM LAST CHRISTMAS!
NOTES
Guisewite

I STAYED UP ALL NIGHT, ZENITH, BUT I **DID** IT! YOU HAVE A HALLOWEEN COSTUME LOVINGLY MADE BY YOUR MOM!
WHERE'S THE OFFICIAL DISNEY TAG?
MILK

I MADE IT MYSELF, HONEY! THERE'S NO TAG.
IF IT DOESN'T HAVE THE DISNEY TAG, IT'S NOT THE REAL ONE.

NOT REAL?? IT'S HOMEMADE! HAND-STITCHED BY MAMA!
COPYRIGHT INFRINGEMENT! TRADEMARK VIOLATION! ILLEGAL FACSIMILE!!
MILK

I'VE CREATED A MONSTER, GUS.
WHERE'S THE OFFICIAL TAG?
MILK
Guisewite

BRIANA'S MOMMY MADE 35 GOBLIN COOKIES AND WROTE EACH CHILD'S NAME ON THE TOP WITH SPARKLY FROSTING...
HAPPY HALLOWEEN

JUSTIN'S MOMMY CARVED "I LOVE YOU" INTO 35 TEENY PUMPKINS...
ASHLEY'S MOMMY BAKED 35 HALLOWEEN TARTS...

AND ZENITH'S MOMMY...
WILL BE RIGHT BACK. SHE HAD TO RUN OUT TO HER CAR...
HAPPY HALLOWEEN

I SAID, JACK-O'-LANTERN CUPCAKES! I NEED 35 JACK-O'-LANTERN CUPCAKES!!
THIS IS A SELF-SERVE GAS STATION, MA'AM.
PAY BEFORE PUMPING
Guisewite

THE KIDS COULDN'T GET ENOUGH OF HALLOWEEN! THEY DRAGGED ME UP AND DOWN THE STREET BEGGING FOR MORE CANDY...

...PLASTERED EVERY WINDOW IN THE HOUSE WITH PUMPKIN STICKERS...GLUED PLASTIC SPIDERS TO EVERY PLATE IN THE CUPBOARD...
UP
DOWN

...PULLED THEIR COSTUMES ON AND OFF SIX TIMES...WATCHED TWO MONSTER VIDEOS... HAD FOUR FIGHTS OVER THE CANDY ...AND NAILED MY HUSBAND'S SUIT WITH PURPLE SLIME!
YOU MUST HAVE BEEN EXHAUSTED LAST NIGHT!

THAT WAS ALL THIS MORNING BEFORE BREAKFAST.
TEN LIFETIMES LIVED IN THE TIME IT TOOK ME TO APPLY MASCARA.

I DON'T WANT YOU TO GO TO WORK, MOMMY!
OH, BABY, I'M SO SORRY...

WHY AM I WORKING?? DO I **HAVE** TO WORK? COULD WE POSSIBLY MAKE IT IF I **DIDN'T** WORK? WILL I ALWAYS REGRET THIS TIME WORKING? IS THERE ANY WAY I COULD WORK **LESS**? DO I HAVE TO WORK?? **WHY AM I WORKING? WHY? WHY?**

I DON'T WANT YOU TO GO TO WORK, DADDY!
DON'T BE SILLY, HONEY. OF COURSE I'M GOING TO WORK.

IS THERE ANYTHING MORE ANNOYING THAN WITNESSING INNER PEACE?

BRIANA'S MOM MADE A HALLOWEEN PARTY MEMORY BOOK FOR EACH KID IN OUR CLASS.
BRIANA'S MOM DOESN'T HAVE A JOB, ZENITH.

JACK'S MOM SAYS RAISING CHILDREN IS THE MOST IMPORTANT JOB IN THE WORLD. SHE EMBROIDERED ALL OUR NAMES ONTO A STORYTIME QUILT.
JACK'S FAMILY DOESN'T NEED THE INCOME.

CARLY'S MOM MADE A MURAL FOR OUR CLASS OUT OF 5,000 PASTA SHELLS... **SAM'S** MOM VIDEOED THE WHOLE MONTH OF SEPTEMBER AND EDITED IT TO THE SOUNDTRACK OF "THE LION KING"...
YOU KNOW WHY I WORK, DON'T YOU, HONEY?

CAN'T TAKE THE COMPETITION AT PRESCHOOL.
NEED TIME AWAY FROM YOU TO THINK UP ANSWERS.

DADDY SAID WE COULD EAT HALLOWEEN CANDY BEFORE DINNER!
I'M TOO TIRED TO ARGUE.

DADDY SAID WE COULD DUMP OUT ALL YOUR DRAWERS AND WATCH AS MANY VIDEOS AS WE LIKE!
I'M TOO TIRED TO PUT UP A FIGHT.

DADDY SAID WE COULD PRETTY MUCH DO ANYTHING WE WANT IF IT'S NOT LIFE THREATENING AND DOESN'T MAKE NOISE!
I'M TOO TIRED TO TAKE A STAND.

NO WONDER THEY CALL THIS "QUALITY TIME".

TO DO, 1955:
1. MARRY WELL.

TO DO, 1975:

1. TRANSFORM ROLE OF WOMEN IN SOCIETY.

TO DO, 1995:

1. EARN LIVING.
2. BUY, FURNISH AND MAINTAIN HOME.
3. PAY ALL BILLS.
4. DO ALL LAUNDRY.
5. BUY ALL GROCERIES.
6. COOK ALL MEALS.
7. LOCATE AND MARRY HUSBAND.
8. HAVE AND RAISE CHILDREN.
9. TONE ALL MUSCLES.
10. REBEL AGAINST AGING.
11. SAVE PLANET.
12. BUY AND MAINTAIN AUTOMOBILE.
13. FIGHT AGAINST EVIL.
14. TAKE CHARGE OF LIFE.
15. GO INTO THERAPY TO REGAIN VULNERABILITY.

I AM WOMAN. HEAR ME SNORE.

IF MY LEGS ARE FAT THIS MORNING, I'LL WEAR THE BROWN PANTS AND JACKET...

IF MY CALVES AND THIGHS ARE GOOD, BUT MY WAIST IS FLABBY, I'LL WEAR THE SHORT TANK DRESS... IF MY STOMACH'S FLAT, BUT THE REAR IS BAD, I'LL WEAR THE LONG SKIRT AND TUNIC...

IF IT'S **ALL** WRONG, I'LL GO WITH THE BAGGY BLACK SUIT AND PRAY FOR A MIRACLE IN THE HAIR DEPARTMENT!

MEN FACE THE DAY. WOMEN GREET A SURPRISE PARTY.
PAT
PAT

CASUAL BLACK FLATS... DRESSY BLACK FLATS... CASUAL AND DRESSY PLATFORM BLACK FLATS...

BLACK STILETTO HEEL... BLACK OPEN-TOED, MEDIUM WEDGE HEEL... BLACK CLOSE-TOED, MEDIUM POINTY HEEL... BLACK SLING-BACK, STRAPPY SHORT HEEL...

...NO BLACK CHUNKY HIGH HEEL, ROUND-TOED, SLIGHT PLATFORM LACE-UPS! THE OUTFIT IS USELESS WITHOUT THE BLACK CHUNKY HIGH HEEL, ROUND-TOED SLIGHT PLATFORM LACE-UPS!

IF DOG IS WOMAN'S BEST FRIEND, IT'S BECAUSE WE CAN'T SAY ANYTHING.

VISUALIZE!
PRIORITIZE!
FOCUS!
ATTACK!
VISUALIZE!
PRIORITIZE!
FOCUS!
ATTACK!

...YES, MOM, I JUST WALKED IN THE DOOR AND I'M VERY...
CATHY

OH, I KNOW YOU'RE BUSY, SWEETIE. I JUST CALLED TO SAY I LOVE YOU AND MISS YOU AND THAT NOTHING ON EARTH WOULD MAKE SENSE TODAY IF I COULDN'T HEAR YOUR BEAUTIFUL VOICE.

A HALF-HOUR MOTIVATIONAL TAPE ONE-UPPED BY FIVE SECONDS WITH MOTHER.

HOW WAS YOUR WEEKEND?
FINE, UNTIL A PRE-THANKSGIVING PIE EPISODE WITH MY MOTHER.

GOOD UNTIL A SUNDAY AFTERNOON RUN-IN WITH A COOKIE EMPORIUM.
PERFECT UNTIL I ACCIDENTALLY ORDERED AND ATE A CHINESE DINNER FOR FOUR.

GREAT UNTIL I STOPPED FOR A FAT-FREE CAFFE LATTE AND EMERGED WITH A 3,000-CALORIE CHOCOLATE CHIP SCONE.

..AND SO, DRAPED IN BLACK, WE BEGIN ANOTHER MONDAY MORNING FUNERAL FOR THE DIET.
DID ANYONE BRING ANY FOOD?...

IGNORE A BOYFRIEND, AND HE WILL DISAPPEAR.

IGNORE A GIRLFRIEND, AND SHE WILL DISAPPEAR. IGNORE CLIENTS, AND THEY WILL DISAPPEAR.
PHONE

IGNORE FAT, AND IT PUTS DOWN ROOTS, SETS UP CAMP, BUILDS A VILLAGE AND STAKES A CLAIM ON YOUR BEING FOR ALL OF ETERNITY.

DO I CURSE THE SYSTEM FOR LETTING ME DOWN, OR REJOICE THAT I FINALLY INSPIRED SOME LOYALTY?
Guisewite

THE MEDICAL REPORT: THE RESULTS OF ANY WEIGHT-LOSS PROGRAM WILL BE GREATLY ENHANCED BY DRINKING 8 GLASSES OF WATER A DAY, 7 DAYS A WEEK, 52 WEEKS A YEAR.

THE HUMAN REPORT: FAT FLOATS.
Guisewite

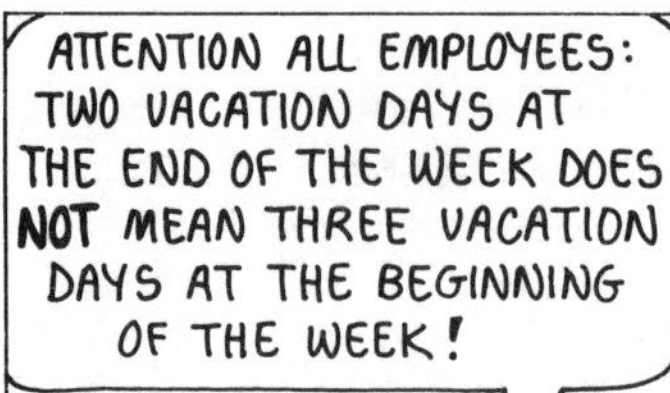

ATTENTION ALL EMPLOYEES: TWO VACATION DAYS AT THE END OF THE WEEK DOES NOT MEAN THREE VACATION DAYS AT THE BEGINNING OF THE WEEK!

TWO VACATION DAYS MEANS YOU HAVE THREE DAYS TO DO FIVE DAYS OF WORK!!

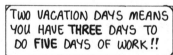

YOU SHOULD BE PANICKED! YOU SHOULD BE WORKING AS FAST AS YOUR LITTLE FINGERS CAN FLY! ANY QUESTIONS?!

WHAT SIZE TURKEY DO I BUY TO FEED NINE PEOPLE?
I HAVE AN AUDIENCE. NOW ALL I NEED IS A LISTENER.
Guisewite

DO YOU THINK THE WEEK BEFORE THANKSGIVING IS A REALISTIC TIME TO START A NEW WEIGHT-LOSS PROGRAM?
I DO.

DO YOU ACTUALLY BELIEVE YOU CAN UNDO THE EATING HABITS OF THE LAST THREE DECADES IN ONE WEEK?
I DO.

DO YOU EXPECT THE WILL-POWER THAT'S ELUDED YOU YOUR WHOLE LIFE TO NOT ONLY SUDDENLY APPEAR, BUT TO CARRY YOU THROUGH THE MOST EMOTIONALLY TRAUMA-TIC, FATTENING-FOOD-FILLED SEASON OF THE YEAR???
I DO.

EVEN WHEN A MOTHER SUSPECTS THE RELATIONSHIP IS HOPELESS, SHE CAN'T HELP BUT WEEP AT THE VOWS.
Guisewite

I'M NOT GOING TO LET MY MOTHER GET TO ME THIS THANKSGIVING.
ME EITHER.

WHEN SHE CRITICIZES MY HOUSE-KEEPING, I'LL HEAR IT AS AN EXPRES-SION OF LOVE.
WHEN SHE COUNTS HOW MANY ROLLS I EAT, I'LL SMILE AND COMPLIMENT HER MATH.
WHEN SHE PICKS AT MY HUSBAND, I'LL THANK HER FOR WANT-ING THE BEST FOR ME.

SHE WON'T GET TO ME THIS YEAR! SHE WILL NOT GET TO ME!!

...SHE GOT TO ME.
NO MATTER HOW FAR AHEAD WE PLAN, THEY'RE ALWAYS ONE STEP AHEAD OF US...
GUISEWITE

IS ALEX COMING FOR THANKSGIVING, CATHY?
MOM, I BROKE UP WITH ALEX LAST FEBRUARY.
CATHY
IN

OH, I KNOW, BUT THINGS MIGHT HAVE REKINDLED.
REKINDLED?? THERE'S NOTHING TO REKINDLE!

WHY DON'T YOU GIVE HIM A CALL?
WHAT ARE YOU TALKING ABOUT, MOTHER?? I'M NOT INVITING AN EX-BOYFRIEND FOR THANKS-GIVING!!

WAS THAT REALLY NECES-SARY?
THE DINNER IS ALWAYS JUICIER IF YOU START THINGS SIMMER-ING THE DAY BEFORE.
GUISEWITE

LEAN TURKEY BREAST FOR LOW-FAT PROTEIN... WHITE POTATOES FOR POTASSIUM...

SWEET POTATOES AND PUMP-KIN FOR BETA CAROTENE... CRANBERRIES FOR VITAMIN A ... GREEN BEANS FOR VITA-MIN C AND ANTIOXIDANTS...

...AND WHIPPED CREAM, BUTTER, GRAVY AND MARSH-MALLOWS JUST BECAUSE WE FEEL LIKE IT.

THE GREAT CHEFS ALL SPEAK TWO LANGUAGES.
GUISEWITE

ANYONE HAVE ROOM FOR A DAB OF SWEET POTATOES?

SURE.

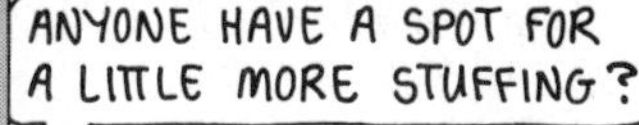
ANYONE HAVE A SPOT FOR A LITTLE MORE STUFFING?

GOT IT.

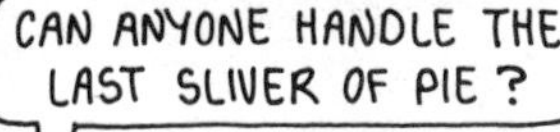
CAN ANYONE HANDLE THE LAST SLIVER OF PIE?

SEND IT OVER.

SOMETIMES I FEEL LIKE A TUPPERWARE CONTAINER WITH NO LID.

DETAILED LIST OF ALL GIFTS NEEDED, INCLUDING PRECISE BUDGET FOR EACH.
CHECK!
GIFTS

MAP OF MALL WITH EXACT SHOPPING ROUTE INDICATED BY PATH OF RED ARROWS.
CHECK!
MALL

CROSS-REFERENCED NOTE-BOOK OF COMPARISON PRICES WITH ALPHABETIZED POCKETS FOR RECEIPTS.
CHECK!

ON THE BRINK OF BATTLE, ANOTHER SQUADRON SURRENDERS TO THE SHOE DEPARTMENT.
CASH OR CHARGE?
CHECK.

HOW COULD I HAVE EATEN SO MUCH?? LOOK AT ME!
ARE YOU KIDDING?? YOU LOOK GREAT! I HAVE FIVE NEW POUNDS TO LOSE!

YOU JUST CAN'T SEE MY FAT BECAUSE I'M WEARING THIS BAGGY JACKET!
HAH! I'M WEARING A BAGGY JACKET, TOO, AND YOU CAN SEE MY FAT ANYWAY!

YOU CAN-NOT!
CAN TOO! LOOK AT THIS! I'M WAY WORSE THAN YOU!

FROM THE INNER SANCTUM OF THE LADIES' ROOM, THE BIZARRE PRIDE OF THE POST-THANKSGIVING WOMAN...
I'M WORSE!
NO! I'M WORSE!
NO! I'M WORSE!
NO! I'M WORSE!
LADIES

...AND WHEN YOU LOCATE **THAT**, I'LL BUY THIS NICE SWEATER TO GO WITH HIM.

WHAT DID YOU DO FOR LUNCH, CATHY?
I DROVE TO THE MALL... RAN THROUGH ALL THREE FLOORS...

...NARROWED 42,000 POTENTIAL GIFTS DOWN TO 1500 SOLID POSSIBILITIES... BOUGHT A ROBE FOR MOM... TRIED ON 14 NEW YEAR'S EVE OUTFITS... FOUND MOM'S NEW ROBE FOR 30% OFF AT A DIFFERENT STORE ON LEVEL ONE...

...RETURNED THE FIRST ROBE ON LEVEL THREE... READ 400 CHRISTMAS CARDS... TRIED ON SIX PAIRS OF BOOTS... AND STOPPED AT THE CLEANERS AND THE MONEY MACHINE.
BUT WHAT DID YOU DO FOR **LUNCH**??

MAN CANNOT LIVE BY BREAD ALONE, BUT WOMAN CAN CONQUER THE WORLD FUELED ONLY BY A RICE CAKE AND A DIET SODA.

IF I CAN GET MY CHRISTMAS CARDS IN THE MAIL TODAY, I'LL BE AHEAD FOR ONCE IN MY LIFE, MOM!

DID YOU BUY THE CARDS?
NO.
CHOOSE THE CARDS?
NO.
ADDRESS ENVELOPES?
NO.
BUY STAMPS?
NO.
COUNT HOW MANY YOU NEED?
NO.

IT'S 9:30 AT NIGHT, CATHY.
I KNOW. IF I CAN GET MY CHRISTMAS CARDS IN THE MAIL TODAY I'LL BE AHEAD FOR ONCE IN MY LIFE!

MY DAUGHTER: THE ENERGIZER BATTERY OF HOPE.

THREE WEEKS BEFORE CHRISTMAS, AND THE MALLS ARE BUSIER THAN THEY'VE BEEN IN A DECADE.

HAS THE RECESSION FINALLY LOST ITS GRIP?? HAS THE SPELL FINALLY BEEN LIFTED??

...OR DOES THE RETURN TO THE MALL SPEAK TO SOME DEEPER CALLING WITHIN THE HUMAN SPIRIT?

I JUST WANT TO BE SOMEPLACE WHERE THE CLOTHES ARE ALL IRONED, THE DISHES ARE ALL CLEAN, AND EVERYTHING ELSE IS STACKED NEATLY ON A NICE, DUSTED SHELF.

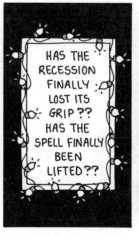

HOW ABOUT THIS GORGEOUS NECKLACE FOR YOUR MOTHER?
Jewelry

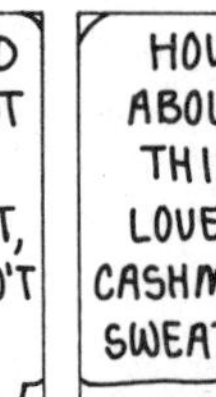
OH, NO. SHE'D SAY I SPENT TOO MUCH MONEY ON IT, AND COULDN'T ENJOY IT.

HOW ABOUT THIS LOVELY CASHMERE SWEATER?
OH, NO. SHE'D SAY IT'S TOO NICE TO USE AND KEEP IT WRAPPED UP IN A DRAWER.
Cashmere

I'M WILLING TO SPEND ANY AMOUNT... BUT FOR **MOM** TO BE HAPPY, THE GIFT HAS TO LOOK INEXPENSIVE AND ORDINARY, WITHOUT- OF COURSE- LOOKING CHEAP AND UGLY.... ALSO, IN SPITE OF THE FACT THAT I'VE SPENT A WEEK SHOPPING FOR IT, IT CAN'T LOOK AS THOUGH IT TOOK A LOT OF TIME TO FIND.

SAY WHAT WE WILL ABOUT MEN, MOTHERS ARE ALWAYS OUR BIGGEST CHALLENGE.
GUISEWITE

YOUR TWO-DAY-ONLY SALE WAS FOLLOWED BY YOUR 24-HOUR SALE... FOLLOWED BY YOUR MIDNIGHT MADNESS SALE...
FINAL HOLIDAY SALE

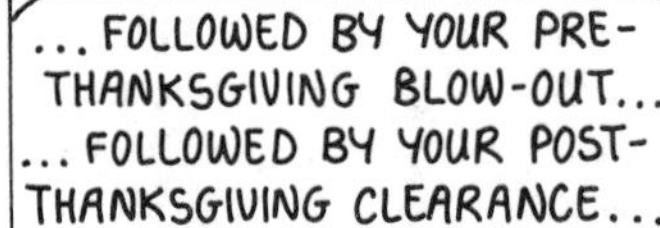
... FOLLOWED BY YOUR PRE-THANKSGIVING BLOW-OUT... ... FOLLOWED BY YOUR POST-THANKSGIVING CLEARANCE...

FINAL HOLIDAY SALE

WHY SHOULD I BUY TODAY? I KNOW YOU'LL SLASH THE PRICES AGAIN! I'M ABSOLUTELY, POSITIVELY SURE YOU'LL HAVE ANOTHER SALE TOMORROW!
HOLIDAY SALE

CURSES. WE'VE CREATED ANOTHER BELIEVER.
IT ALWAYS HAPPENS DURING THE HOLIDAYS.
GUISEWITE

EVERYONE ELSE IS CARRYING BAGS OF PRESENTS... EVERYONE ELSE HAS MADE DECISIONS..
SHOPS
Happy Holidays
Happy Holidays

EVERYONE ELSE KNOWS WHAT THEY'RE DOING... EVERYONE ELSE IS MORE ORGANIZED AND EFFICIENT... EVERYONE ELSE IS HAPPIER... EVERYONE ELSE IS FULL OF HOLIDAY JOY...
SHOPS

WAAH!!

HOW'D YOU DO AT THE MALL?
NO ACTUAL GIFTS, BUT I GOT FIVE CHOCOLATE SANTAS SHIPPED OFF TO MY STOMACH.
RECEPTION
GUISEWITE

"TO AVOID HOLIDAY WEIGHT GAIN, EAT A SMALL, NUTRITIOUS MEAL BEFORE GOING TO A PARTY".
Holiday

"TO AVOID HOLIDAY WEIGHT GAIN, SUBSTITUTE CRUNCHY VEGGIES FOR FATTENING HORS D'OEUVRES."
Holiday

"TO AVOID HOLIDAY WEIGHT GAIN, PARTAKE OF LIVELY CONVERSATION, NOT EGG NOG."
Holiday

COFFEE ROOM RULES

NO AMOUNT OF MAGAZINE ARTICLES CAN PREPARE US FOR WHAT'S LURKING IN THE COFFEE ROOM.
Guisewite

YOUR FATHER AND I AREN'T USING ANY CHARGE CARDS THIS CHRISTMAS, CATHY.
WHY ARE YOU TELLING ME THIS, MOM?
Menu
Menu

NO REASON. WE THOUGHT, WHY NOT JUST BUY WHAT WE CAN AFFORD WITH CASH AND SKIP THE HUGE CREDIT CARD DEBT?
IF YOU'RE TRYING TO GIVE ME ADVICE, JUST GIVE IT, MOM. DON'T PRETEND YOU'RE NOT DOING IT!

I WAS SIMPLY MAKING CONVERSATION.
DROP THE CHARADE, MOTHER! JUST GIVE ME ADVICE AND GET IT OVER WITH!

ALL IT TAKES IS A LITTLE PLANNING FOR EVERY MOTHER'S DREAM TO COME TRUE.
GIVE ME ADVICE! PLEASE! JUST GIVE ME ADVICE!!

...OH, NO. I JUST MET HER FIVE MINUTES AGO AND I CAN'T REMEMBER HER NAME!
Happy Holidays

...AACK! I'VE KNOWN HIM FOR SIX YEARS AND I CAN'T REMEMBER HIS NAME!
Happy Holidays

...I KNOW THEM, BUT FROM WHERE?? WHO ARE THEY?? WHAT ARE THEIR NAMES??
Happy Holidays

AS AMNESIA FOR ALL HUMANS SETS IN, ANOTHER HOLIDAY PARTY-GOER SEEKS OUT THE FAMILIAR FACE OF THE HORS D'OEUVRES PLATTER.

...WAIT. I ALREADY GOT THIS CATALOG. IT JUST HAD A DIFFERENT COVER.
GIFTS

IN FACT, I GET A NEW VERSION OF THIS EXACT SAME CATALOG EVERY WEEK WITH A DIFFERENT COVER.
GIFTS

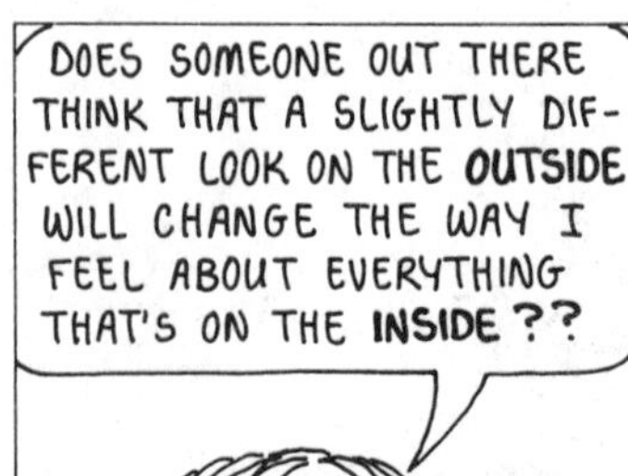
DOES SOMEONE OUT THERE THINK THAT A SLIGHTLY DIFFERENT LOOK ON THE **OUTSIDE** WILL CHANGE THE WAY I FEEL ABOUT EVERYTHING THAT'S ON THE **INSIDE**??

GIFTS

WELL, YES, ACTUALLY. WE'VE BASED MOST OF OUR LIFE ON THAT CONCEPT.
THAT'S DIFFERENT. WITH THE PROPER NEW OUTFIT, I **AM** DIFFERENT ON THE INSIDE.

YOU KNOW HOW YOU AND I NEVER EXCHANGE CHRISTMAS GIFTS, CATHY?
YES! OUR UNSPOKEN PACT! THE TRADITION OF NON-GIVING! A COMPLETE, GUILT-FREE RELIEF!

I WAS SO GRATEFUL, I GOT YOU A LITTLE SOMETHING THIS YEAR.
AACK!! THE "TOKEN OF APPRECIATION FOR NOT HAVING TO GET YOU ANYTHING GIFT"! NEW CATEGORY! AACK!!

SORRY.
IS THERE NO ONE LEFT WITH WHOM I CAN BE COMPLETELY THOUGHTLESS??
GUISEWITE

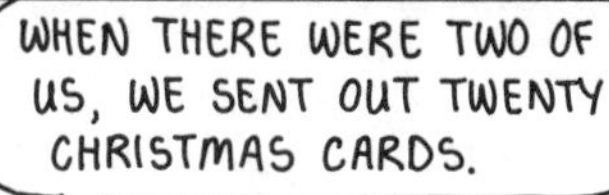
WHEN THERE WERE TWO OF US, WE SENT OUT TWENTY CHRISTMAS CARDS.

ADDRESS BOOK
CARDS

NOW THERE ARE FOUR OF US. BETWEEN DAY CARE, PRESCHOOL, PLAY GROUPS AND NEIGHBORS, EACH CHILD HAS 63 FRIENDS. EACH FRIEND HAS TWO PARENTS, SOME OF WHOM LIVE AT TWO DIFFERENT ADDRESSES.

BY ADDING TWO TINY PEOPLE TO OUR FAMILY, WE'VE ADDED 350 NAMES TO OUR CHRISTMAS CARD LIST.

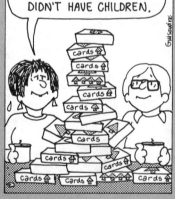

WHOEVER SAID IT WAS A SMALL WORLD OBVIOUSLY DIDN'T HAVE CHILDREN.
GUISEWITE

DID YOU EVER CALL THE WILSONS ABOUT...
I KNOW! THE WREATH THEY SENT! I CAN'T DEAL WITH THAT THIS WEEK, MOM!
DO

THE MONROES SAID THEY NEVER HEARD FROM...
I KNOW! I MISSED THEIR HOLIDAY PARTY! I OWE THEM A NOTE OF APOLOGY!
DO

ALSO, DAD WONDERS ABOUT...
IT'S ON THE LIST! I HAVE A LIST OF ALL HIDEOUS OVERSIGHTS AND WILL DEAL WITH THEM ALL WHEN I COME TO YOUR HOUSE FOR CHRISTMAS!!
DO

I ALWAYS FEEL BETTER ABOUT HER MAKING THE GUILT TRIP IF I KNOW SHE'S MADE THE GUILT RESERVATIONS.

GUISEWITE

PINK STICKERS ON THINGS I PROBABLY WANT TO ORDER... GREEN STICKERS ON THINGS I MIGHT WANT TO ORDER...

BLUE STICKERS ON THINGS I WANT BUT THINK I SAW A BETTER VERSION OF IN ANOTHER CATALOG... CORNERS FOLDED OVER WHERE I RAN OUT OF STICKERS... CHECKS ON CATALOGS WHICH HAVE ABSOLUTELY NOTHING I WANT, BUT WHICH I MIGHT WANT TO LOOK THROUGH AGAIN....

HELLO. I'D LIKE TO ORDER A HUMAN BEING TO DO MY CHRISTMAS SHOPPING FOR ME.

OUT OF STOCK?? YOU CAN'T BE OUT OF STOCK!
YOU SHOULDN'T HAVE WAITED UNTIL THE LAST MINUTE TO ORDER.

I **DIDN'T**. YOUR CATALOG SAYS, "ORDER BY DECEMBER 22, DELIVERY BY **CHRISTMAS**". ... AND IT DOESN'T JUST SAY IT IN **ONE** PLACE. IT SAYS IT ON ALL **200 PAGES**! IT **SCREAMS** IT ON THE COVER!

YOUR CATALOG PRACTICALLY BEGS ME TO WAIT UNTIL DECEMBER 22, AND I **DIDN'T**! IT'S ONLY DECEMBER **18**!! I'M ORDERING **EARLY** THIS YEAR, I TELL YOU!! **I AM ORDERING EARLY!!**

CLICK

FOR THE ONE I LOVE: A PHOTO OF ITEM #487Q WRAPPED IN A FALSE SENSE OF SECURITY.

SHE CAN EXCHANGE IT IF IT DOESN'T FIT.
IF SHE EXCHANGES IT, SHE'LL KNOW I GOT IT FOR 60% OFF.
Holiday Blow-out 60% OFF

IT'S A LOVELY GIFT!
IT'S A LOVELY GIFT IF SHE THINKS I SPENT $40 ON IT... ... IT'S NOT NEARLY AS LOVELY IF SHE FINDS OUT IT WAS ON THE $15.99 CLEARANCE RACK.

IT'S STILL A $40 VALUE!
BUT IF SHE ACTUALLY SPENDS $40 ON MY GIFT, THIS GIFT IS INFERIOR... AND IF SHE BUYS ME A $15.99 GIFT, THIS GIFT IS TOO NICE.

SALES TO THE PUBLIC WOULD GO SO MUCH BETTER IF THERE WEREN'T ANY HUMANS INVOLVED.
Holiday Blow-out 60% OFF

OUT OF MY WAY! I'M TRYING TO DO A MONTH OF CHRISTMAS SHOPPING ON MY LUNCH HOUR!

EVERYONE WHO DOESN'T HAVE TO GET BACK TO AN OFFICE, GO HOME! YOU HAVE ALL DAY TO SHOP! I HAVE 35 MINUTES! HURRY! HURRY! I HAVE TO GET BACK! I HAVE TO GET BACK!

I'M BACK! I TRAMPLED, SHOVED, YELLED AND OFFENDED, BUT I'M BACK! I MADE IT BACK TO THE OFFICE!
YAWN
TWEET
SCARF

...AND AM MARCHING DIRECTLY TO THE LADIES' ROOM AND SEEING IF I CAN SNEAK OUT THROUGH A WINDOW...
Guisewite

WE LIVE IN THE SAME TOWN, MOM. WHY DO I NEED TO PACK A SUITCASE AND DISRUPT YOUR WHOLE HOME BY MOVING IN WITH YOU FOR CHRISTMAS?
YOU DON'T NEED TO DO THAT IF YOU DON'T WANT TO, CATHY.

I ALWAYS DO IT BECAUSE I THOUGHT YOU WANTED ME TO.
I ONLY WANT YOU TO IF YOU WANT TO. I HOPE YOU DIDN'T DO IT ALL THESE YEARS JUST BECAUSE I WANT YOU TO.

OF COURSE I WANT TO, TOO, MOM.
GREAT. IF YOU WANT TO THEN I WANT YOU TO.

ANOTHER ROCK-SOLID FAMILY TRADITION BUILT ON A SWAMP OF WILL.
Guisewite

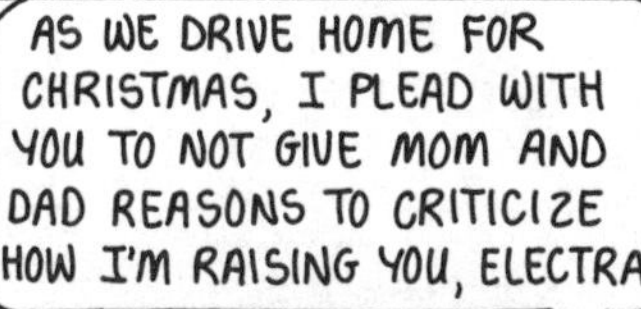
AS WE DRIVE HOME FOR CHRISTMAS, I PLEAD WITH YOU TO NOT GIVE MOM AND DAD REASONS TO CRITICIZE HOW I'M RAISING YOU, ELECTRA.

NO BEGGING. NO YAPPING. NO CHEWING. NO ACCIDENTS. MAKE IT THROUGH THIS VISIT WITH A SHRED OF SELF-CONTROL, AND YOU WILL HAVE MY ETERNAL GRATITUDE AND DEVOTION!

GRANDMA HAS A COOKIE!!
YAP YAP YAP

YOU'RE PITIFUL.
AS THOUGH YOU HAVEN'T SWITCHED ALLEGIANCES FOR LESS.
TSK. YOUR MOM STILL HASN'T TAUGHT YOU TO NOT JUMP.
Guisewite

DON'T LOAD UP ON FOOD, SWEETIE. WE'RE GOING OUT TO A BIG CHRISTMAS DINNER.
CHRISTMAS DINNER IS TWO DAYS AWAY, MOM. I'M EATING ONE PIECE OF TOAST.

I JUST DON'T WANT YOU TO FILL UP.
STARVING YOURSELF FOR TWO DAYS BEFORE A HUGE MEAL IS THE WORST POSSIBLE THING YOU CAN DO.

THERE'S NOTHING WRONG WITH EATING ONE PIECE OF TOAST! THERE'S NOTHING WRONG WITH TWO PIECES OF TOAST! I COULD EAT A WHOLE LOAF OF TOAST IF I WANTED, AND I THINK I WILL!!
BREAD

I SEE SHE FELL FOR THE 8:00 AM MOTHERLY CHALLENGE.
THE GAMES WE HAVE TO PLAY TO GET OUR CHILDREN TO EAT...
Guisewite

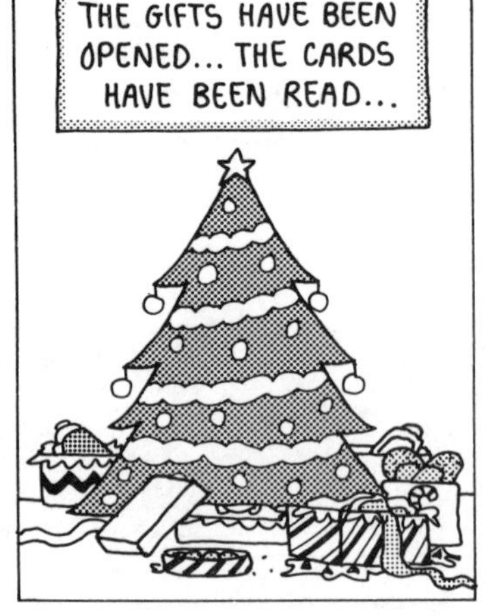
THE GIFTS HAVE BEEN OPENED... THE CARDS HAVE BEEN READ...

THE RELATIVES HAVE BEEN CALLED... THE DINNER'S BEEN EATEN...

AROUND THE COUNTRY, FAMILIES SIT TOGETHER AND QUIETLY SHARE ONE POIGNANT, UNSPOKEN THOUGHT...

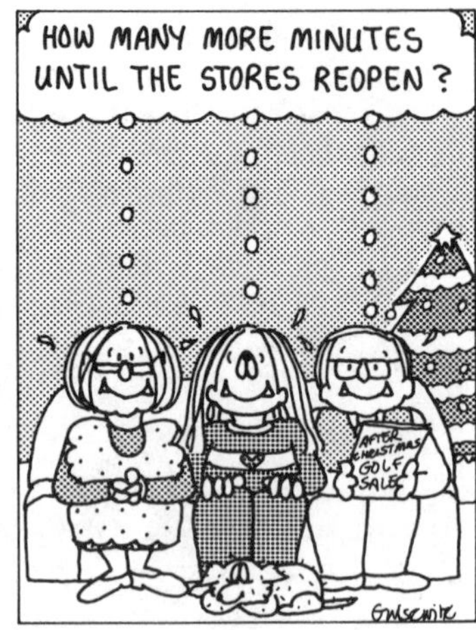
HOW MANY MORE MINUTES UNTIL THE STORES REOPEN?
AFTER CHRISTMAS GOLF SALE
Guisewite

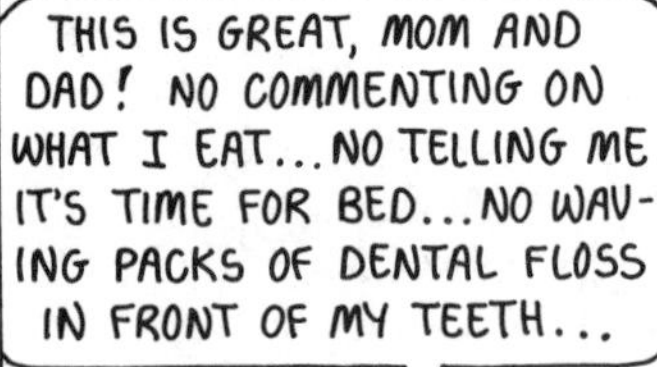
THIS IS GREAT, MOM AND DAD! NO COMMENTING ON WHAT I EAT... NO TELLING ME IT'S TIME FOR BED... NO WAVING PACKS OF DENTAL FLOSS IN FRONT OF MY TEETH...

A FULL EVENING'S PASSED WITH NO MENTION OF MY LOVE LIFE, MY FINANCES, MY DOG'S MANNERS OR MY HAIR.

I'M AN ADULT! YOU'RE TREATING ME LIKE AN ADULT! LOOK AT ME! I'M AN OFFICIAL ADULT!

IT'S BEST TO JUST NOD AND ACT AGREEABLE WHEN SHE GETS OVERTIRED.
Guisewite

YOU MUST BE MARTHA'S NEPHEW. THIS IS MY DAUGHTER. SHE'S SINGLE!
Happy Holidays

NEVER MARRIED! COMPLETELY UNATTACHED! PERFECTLY SINGLE!
Happy Holidays

NOT DESPERATE! JUST SINGLE! SINGLE, SINGLE, SINGLE!

HELLO. I'M CATHY, AND THIS IS MY ALTAR EGO.
Happy Holidays

MAYBE IF YOU KIND OF WALKED PAST HIM HE'D...
I CAN BE BOLD, MOM...

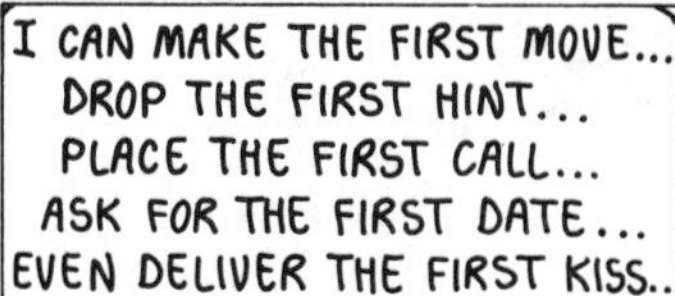
I CAN MAKE THE FIRST MOVE... DROP THE FIRST HINT... PLACE THE FIRST CALL... ASK FOR THE FIRST DATE... EVEN DELIVER THE FIRST KISS..

I CAN TAKE THE INITIATIVE WITH GRACE, CONFIDENCE AND CHARM... BUT I AM NOT GOING TO DO IT WITH HIM, MOTHER!! I AM NOT WASTING IT ON HIM!!!

GET OUR COATS, DEAR. I'VE JUST UNLEASHED TWENTY YEARS OF ASSERTIVENESS TRAINING ONTO HELEN'S DESSERT TABLE.

REMEMBER HOW ORGANIZED I WAS WHEN I GOT HERE, MOM? REMEMBER HOW MY CLOTHES WERE ALL ON HANGERS AND MY PURSE ACTUALLY SHUT??

OH, YES, CATHY... AND REMEMBER THAT MY HOUSE WAS SPOTLESS WHEN YOU ARRIVED?? REMEMBER HOW YOU COULD SEE THE KITCHEN COUNTER??

REMEMBER MY LIST OF THINGS TO DO WHILE I WAS HERE??
REMEMBER MY FOLDER OF FUN FAMILY PROJECTS?
REMEMBER OUR PROMISE THAT THIS VISIT WOULDN'T DETERIORATE INTO CHAOS??

FOR MOST PEOPLE, IT TAKES YEARS TO GET NOSTALGIC. FOR MOTHERS AND DAUGHTERS, IT JUST TAKES A COUPLE OF DAYS.

WILL YOU COOK ME A NICE BIG BREAK-FAST BEFORE I GO, MOM?
BREAKFAST?? YOU'LL LET ME FIX YOU BREAK-FAST??

I CAN'T GET MY SUITCASE CLOSED, DAD. WILL YOU HELP?
YOU NEED HELP?? YOU'LL ACTU-ALLY LET ME HELP?
JAM

WILL YOU BRUSH MY HAIR, MOM? WILL YOU TALK TO ME ABOUT MY JOB, DAD? WILL YOU BOTH JUST SIT HERE AND HELP ME FIG-URE OUT MY LIFE??
JAM

SHE'S NEVER SO COM-PLETELY OURS AGAIN AS WHEN SHE'S PREPARING TO WALK OUT THE DOOR.
JAM

NO SNACKS! THE DIET HAS BEGUN!

TODAY DOESN'T COUNT. IT'S A HOLIDAY.

NO SNACKS! THE DIET HAS BEGUN!

TODAY DOESN'T COUNT. IT'S A HOLIDAY.
NO YES NO YES NO NO YES NO NO YES

...AND SO ANOTHER SPECTATOR SETTLES IN FOR BRAIN BOWL '96: THE RESOLUTIONS VS. THE RATIONALIZATIONS.

I GET UP AND GET READY THE EXACT SAME WAY EVERY DAY...

I WORK THE SAME WAY... RELATE TO PEOPLE THE SAME WAY... PLAN TO REFORM THE SAME WAY...

EVERY AREA OF MY LIFE IS A ROUTINE SO FIRMLY ES-TABLISHED THAT THE ROU-TINES HAVE SUB-ROUTINES, AND THE SUB-ROUTINES ARE CREATING THEIR OWN LITTLE SUB-SUB ROUTINES.

I'M STILL UNMARRIED, AND MY RUTS ARE HAVING GRANDCHILDREN.

WHEW! WHAT A NEW YEAR'S! I MUST HAVE HAD SIX CAFFE LATTES! I WAS BUZZED UNTIL 3:00AM!
I HIT THE JAVA PRETTY HARD MYSELF, AND THEN GOT COMPLETELY WASTED ON A BAG OF LOW-SODIUM BEET CHIPS!
I CRASHED UNTIL 10:00AM YESTERDAY, AND THEN DIVED RIGHT BACK INTO THE FAT-FREE, CHOLESTEROL-FREE, NON-DAIRY VEGGIE SAUCE!
I COULD ONLY MAKE IT THROUGH TWO K'S OF MY FIVE-K RUN!
IS THERE ANYTHING MORE SICKENING THAN WITNESSING A HEALTH HANGOVER?
QUIET! I'M STILL HALF IN THE HERBAL TEA BAG.
Guisewite

LAST YEAR! LAST YEAR! LAST YEAR! LAST YEAR!
1995

YOU DIDN'T REALLY LOOK AT ME!
YOU DIDN'T ADD ME UP!
YOU NEVER ANSWERED ME!
YOU STUCK ME IN THE WRONG PLACE!

WHAT?? NOW WHAT?? WHAT IS IT NOW??!
1995

1995 HAS BEEN PUT TO BED, BUT IT'S LYING IN THERE WITH A FLASHLIGHT THINKING UP EXCUSES TO NOT GO TO SLEEP.
1995

FOR 15 YEARS, I'VE TRIED AND FAILED TO LOSE WEIGHT.
FOR 15 YEARS, I'VE BELIEVED THE NEXT DIET WOULD WORK.

FOR 15 YEARS, I'VE ANALYZED EVERY BITE OF FOOD.
FOR 15 YEARS, I'VE BELIEVED IT WOULD MAKE A DIF- FERENCE.

FOR 15 YEARS, EVERY POUND I'VE LOST HAS COME RUNNING BACK HOME TO MY THIGHS.
FOR 15 YEARS, I'VE BELIEVED IT WAS JUST VISITING.

BEHOLD THE BEAUTIFUL BALANCE OF NATURE: THE FAT GENE COEXISTING WITH THE FAITH GENE.

WHAT WAS ONCE A MOST PRIVATE AND PERSONAL AREA OF LIFE HAS BECOME A MULTI-MILLION-DOLLAR BUSINESS.

IT CALLS TO US FROM THE MINI-MALLS... IT BECKONS FROM THE CATALOGS... ...IT HAS A SECTION IN THE VIDEO STORE AND ACRES OF RETAIL SPACE ALL ITS OWN...

IT TANTALIZES AND SEDUCES WITH AN IRRESISTIBLE APPEAL TO OUR MOST PRIMAL INSTINCTS...

GOODBYE, LINGERIE. HELLO, COORDINATED STORAGE SYSTEMS.
LOOK! THERE'S A LITTLE COMPARTMENT FOR EVERY PAIR OF SOCKS!
ORGANIZE

I WANT THE INSIDES OF MY CLOSETS TO BE BEAUTIFUL, BUT I CAN'T DECIDE IF I'M THE POLKA DOT TYPE, THE WOOD GRAIN TYPE OR THE PASTEL PAISLEY TYPE.
STORAGE SYSTEMS

WHAT DOES THE REST OF YOUR HOME REFLECT ?

THE REST OF MY HOME REFLECTS THAT I'M THE "FLING-IT-IN-THE-CLOSET-AND-SHUT-THE-DOOR-BEFORE-IT-ALL-DUMPS-OUT-ON-THE-FLOOR" TYPE.

AH. THE MOOT POINT TYPE.
THE WILLING TO BELIEVE TYPE!
GO WITH THE FLORALS. THEY'LL BE EASIER TO FIND IN THE RUBBLE.
GUISEWITE

PHOTO BOXES THAT MATCH PHOTO ALBUMS THAT MATCH RECEIPT KEEPERS THAT MATCH MAGAZINE HOLDERS!
RECEIP
PHOTOS

STACKING SHOE SHELVES! ROLLING FILE CABINETS! GIFT WRAP ORGANIZERS! JEWELRY COMPARTMENTS! A BAG FOR EVERY SWEATER AND A CUBICLE FOR EVERY PAPER CLIP! **YES!**

I WILL BE ORGANIZED! CHAOS-FREE!! **I AM STAKING A CLAIM ON MY SANITY!!!**
THAT WILL BE $543.00.

WE ALL WANT THE CURE, BUT WHICH OF US IS EVER PREPARED FOR THE THERAPY BILL?
ROLL 'N' FILE
GUISEWITE

HOW COULD YOU SPEND MONEY ON STORAGE SYSTEMS TO SAVE THIS JUNK, CATHY!

IT ISN'T **BAD** JUNK, MOM.

Sort and store

SEE? I'LL PUT THE CUTE LITTLE NOTE CARDS I DON'T USE INTO THAT CUTE LITTLE FILE... I'LL PUT THE NICE LITTLE BROKEN EARRINGS I NEVER WEAR INTO THIS NICE LITTLE BOX... I'LL PUT THE DARLING SAMPLES OF COLOGNE I DON'T LIKE INTO THESE DARLING DRAWERS...

IT'S **CUTE** JUNK, MOM! IT'S **NICE, HARMLESS, CUTE** JUNK!

SHE ISN'T A PACK RAT. SHE'S A PACK GERBIL.
Sort and store
GUISEWITE

IF A MAGAZINE'S MORE THAN A MONTH OLD, GET RID OF IT! IF A NEWSPAPER'S A DAY OLD, THROW IT OUT!
THROW OUT
KEEP

IF YOU HAVEN'T USED A PIECE OF CLOTHING IN SIX MONTHS, GIVE IT AWAY! ... SEE, CATHY?? IT'S ALL ABOUT HAVING A SYSTEM! ORGANIZATION ONLY WORKS IF YOU HAVE A CLEAR, CONCISE SYSTEM!!
THROW OUT
KEEP

SHE OPTED FOR THE "KEEP·THE·DEBRIS·AND·ELIMINATE·THE·MOTHER·FROM·THE·ROOM" SYSTEM.

I RENTED A STORAGE ROOM, MOM!
A STORAGE ROOM FOR WHAT, CATHY?
STORE ALL

A STORAGE ROOM FOR ALL THE STUFF I'M PUTTING IN NICE NEW STORAGE BOXES THAT WON'T FIT IN MY CLOSET.
STORE ALL

YOU BOUGHT TOO MUCH STUFF IN THE FIRST PLACE...YOU CAN'T STAND TO PART WITH IT... AND NOW YOU'RE WRAPPING IT UP IN PRETTY NEW OUTFITS AND RENTING IT A SMALL HOME TO LIVE IN??
STORE ALL

AND YOU THOUGHT MY GENERATION COULDN'T COMMIT!
TO A HUMAN! THE COMMITMENT WAS SUPPOSED TO BE TO A HUMAN!!

THE BOOM IN THE HOME ORGANIZATION BUSINESS IS A DIRECT RESULT OF THE STRESS-FILLED TIMES IN WHICH WE LIVE.

RELATIONSHIPS ARE BIZARRE. BUSINESS IS BERSERK. FINANCES ARE BEYOND COMPREHENSION.
KNOCK KNOCK
RING RING
BEEP!
RING RING

NO WONDER WE LONG FOR NEAT LITTLE BOXES AND MATCHING HANGERS... NO MATTER HOW CHAOTIC THE REST OF THE WORLD IS, A PERSON'S HOME IS THE ONE TINY OASIS WHERE SHE CAN BE IN COMPLETE CONTROL.
HONK HONK HONK HONK

GET IN THOSE ALBUMS, PHOTOS!! PUT YOURSELF IN CHRONOLOGICAL ORDER AND GET IN THOSE ALBUMS!!!
MISC. PHOTOS 1977-1995

IT WILL MAKE YOU FEEL FABULOUS AND LOOK INCREDIBLE.
FITNESS 8000
CHOCOLATE
IT WILL IMPROVE YOUR LOVE LIFE AND YOUR WORK LIFE AND START THE MOMENTUM FOR MIRACULOUS TRANSFORMATIONS THAT WILL AFFECT EVERY REMAINING MOMENT OF YOUR TIME ON EARTH.
FITNESS 8000
IT WILL GIVE YOU THREE SECONDS OF SUPERFICIAL JOY.
CHOCOLATE
I'M TOUGH TO REASON WITH AT 9:00PM.
FITNESS 8000
Guisewite

ON ANDREA'S DESK:
PHOTO OF HUSBAND AND CHILDREN, WHO MAKE IT ALL WORTHWHILE.

ON JIM'S DESK:
PHOTO OF ANNUAL EUROPEAN VACATION, WHICH MAKES IT ALL WORTHWHILE.

ON ROGER'S DESK:
PHOTO OF BEACH-FRONT COTTAGE, WHICH MAKES IT ALL WORTHWHILE.

ON CATHY'S DESK:
PHOTO OF ORGANIZED BATHROOM CABINET, WHICH GIVES HOPE THAT WHOLE LIFE WILL NOW COME INTO ORDER AND THAT HUSBAND, CHILDREN, EUROPEAN VACATION AND BEACH-FRONT COTTAGE WILL FALL INTO PLACE AND MAKE IT ALL WORTHWHILE.

HELP ME, CHARLENE! I CLEANED MY PURSE, AND NOW I CAN'T STOP!
OH, NO! THE PURSE? YOU DID THE PURSE?!!
RECEPTION

WHEN I SAW MY CLEAN PURSE, I HAD TO ORGANIZE MY BATHROOM CABINET... ...WHEN I SAW THE CABINET, I HAD TO DO THE KITCHEN CUPBOARDS...THEN THE SHELVES ...THE CD'S... AND NOW I'M MOVING INTO CLOSETS. HELP!!

TOO LATE! START WITH THE PURSE AND YOU'VE DOOMED YOURSELF TO THE BLACK HOLE OF OBSESSIVE ORGANIZING! NO ONE CAN HELP YOU! THERE'S NO TURNING BACK!
RECEPTION

CURSES! CURSES ON MY NICE, CLEAN PURSE!!
YET ANOTHER REASON WHY MEN DON'T CARRY HANDBAGS.
RECEPTION

WHY DON'T YOU KEEP ONE LITTLE BOX TO FILE ALL COUPONS AND CLIPPINGS ALPHABETICALLY, CATHY?
BECAUSE THAT ISN'T MY SYSTEM, MOM.
COUPONS
NOTES

YOU'VE ONLY OWNED YOUR SYSTEM FOR FOUR DAYS. I'VE BEEN PERFECTING MY SYSTEM FOR 45 YEARS!
YOU'VE BEEN PERFECTING YOUR SYSTEM FOR 45 YEARS, BUT YOU DON'T USE YOUR SYSTEM!

I DON'T USE MY SYSTEM, BUT IT WOULD WORK IF I DID USE IT!
MOTHER, IF I'M GOING TO NOT USE A SYSTEM, I WANT IT TO BE MY OWN SYSTEM! MY OWN, UNIQUE SYSTEM!!

MY DAUGHTER: A RUGGED INDIVIDUALIST WHO'S AN EXACT CLONE OF ME.
COUPONS
NOTES

I NEED ONE MORE PHOTO ALBUM IN THE STAR PATTERN TO COMPLETE MY LIFELONG DREAM OF HAVING A DECADE OF PHOTOS ORGANIZED INTO MATCHING ALBUMS!
Photo Systems

THE STAR PATTERN HAS BEEN DISCON-TINUED.
I CHOSE THE STAR PATTERN BECAUSE IT WAS THE ONE YOU SAID YOU ALWAYS HAD.

WE ALWAYS USED TO HAVE IT, BUT IT WAS DISCONTIN-UED, SO NOW WE DON'T HAVE IT ANYMORE.
I JUST PUT 9½ YEARS IN THE STAR PATTERN! I'M BEG-GING YOU! LET ME FINISH ONE THING IN MY LIFE!!

WE'RE OUT OF THE STAR PATTERN, BUT WE'RE OVER-STOCKED ON BLAME.
IF THE REST OF MY LIFE IS CHAOS, IT'S ALL YOUR FAULT!!!

MAKE THE BED, OR LEAVE IT A MESS? ...HANG UP THE TOWELS, OR THROW THEM ON THE FLOOR?...

THE FIRST DECISIONS OF THE MORNING SET THE PRECEDENT FOR EVERYTHING THAT FOLLOWS.

THE MOMENTUM OF THE WHOLE DAY IS DETERMINED BY THE CHOICES I MAKE BE-FORE I'VE EVEN GOT-TEN TO HAVE MY FIRST CUP OF COFFEE.

GO BACK TO BED AND START OVER, OR GO BACK TO BED AND JUST STAY HERE?

I'VE CALLED THIS SPECIAL MEETING TO ADDRESS THE SINGLE GREATEST CAUSE OF EMPLOYEE ABSENTEEISM...

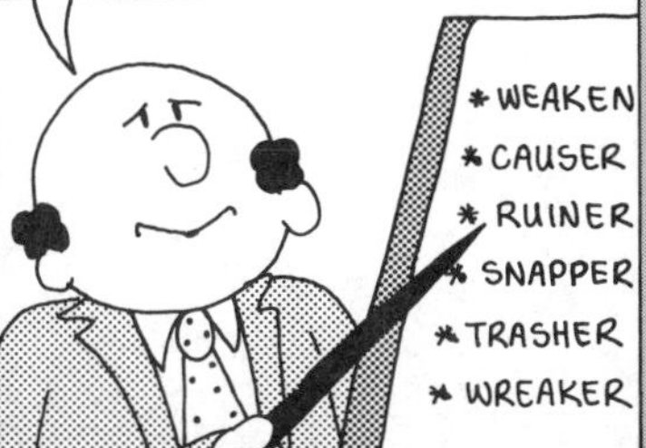
THE WEAKENER OF DEFENSES... CAUSER OF SICKNESS... RUINER OF DIETS... SNAPPER OF BRAIN CELLS... TRASHER OF SELF-CONFIDENCE... WREAKER OF HAVOC...
* WEAKEN
* CAUSER
* RUINER
* SNAPPER
* TRASHER
* WREAKER

IN A WORD, I'M TALKING ABOUT...

MEN!
STRESS!
SAME THING.
STRESS

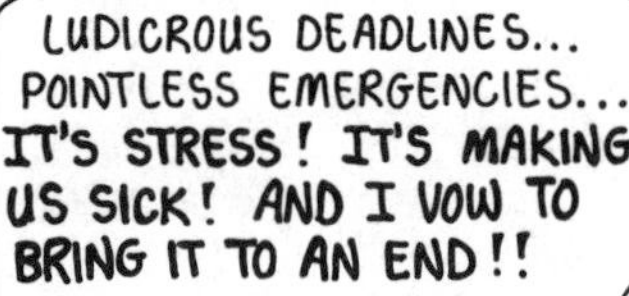
LUDICROUS DEADLINES... POINTLESS EMERGENCIES... IT'S STRESS! IT'S MAKING US SICK! AND I VOW TO BRING IT TO AN END!!

MY 1996 GOAL IS TO CREATE A HAPPY, TRANQUIL ENVIRONMENT WHERE CHEERFUL, HEALTHY FRIENDS WORK SIDE BY SIDE, TAKING PRIDE IN A JOB WELL DONE!

AS A SYMBOL OF MY COMMITMENT, I'VE ASKED CATHY TO GIVE EACH EMPLOYEE A HANDBOOK OF STRESS-REDUCING TIPS AND GUIDELINES.
EVERYONE BUT ME LEFT EARLY WITH THE FLU TODAY, MR. PINKLEY.

MESSENGER THE BOOKLETS TO THEIR HOMES AND HAVE THEM E-MAIL THEIR STRATEGIES BACK BY 4:00 PM!!
I'M FEELING A BIT QUEASY MYSELF...

"TO MANAGE STRESS, SIMPLY QUIT WORRYING SO MUCH."
OH, RIGHT... HA, HA!
COPING SKILLS

HA, HA! AND HERE'S A GOOD ONE!... "TO LOSE WEIGHT, SIMPLY EAT LESS"!
HA, HA, HA! WHO WRITES THIS STUFF?!
COPING SKILLS

HOO, HA, HA!! WHY NOT JUST SAY, "TO LIVE HAPPILY EVER AFTER, SIMPLY MARRY A HANDSOME PRINCE AND RIDE OFF IN HIS HORSE-DRAWN CARRIAGE"??! HA, HA, HA!!

THAT ONE ISN'T FUNNY, CHARLENE!
NEVER JOKE ABOUT ROYALTY WHEN THERE'S A FUTURE PRINCESS IN THE ROOM.

GOOD MORNING, STAFF, AND WELCOME TO YOUR HAPPY, STRESS-FREE WORK ENVIRONMENT!
NO STRESS

WE'LL START TODAY WITH 20 MINUTES OF OXYGENATING STRETCHES... FOLLOWED BY A CHAMOMILE TEA AND FAT-FREE SCONE SNACK... AND THEN WILL BREAK INTO SMALL GROUPS FOR 30 MINUTES OF SPECIAL SHARING.
Scones

BUT FIRST, SINCE LAUGHTER IS THE BEST MEDICINE, PERHAPS SOMEONE CAN START US OFF WITH A JOKE OF THE DAY!

THE BAILEY PRESENTATION HAS TO BE REDONE BY 10:00 AM!

HA HA HOO HOO HA HA!
WAAH!
WEEPING IS ALSO A NATURAL RELAXANT.
NO STRESS

IN LIFE, THERE ARE TWO KINDS OF PEOPLE: THE WHINERS AND THE DOERS.
STRESS MANAGEMENT

WHINERS ARE BEATEN BY STRESS. DOERS USE STRESS IN A HEALTHY, PRODUCTIVE WAY.
STRESS MGMT

WHEN YOU'RE WHINING, YOU DON'T HAVE TIME FOR DOING. WHEN YOU'RE DOING, YOU DON'T HAVE TIME FOR WHINING. SO, TEAM... ARE WE GOING TO BE WHINERS, OR ARE WE GOING TO BE DOERS??!
SHRED SHRED SHRED SHRED

OK. ACTION. I LIKE IT. IT'S A START.
STRESS MANAGEMENT

PROBLEM: OVEREATING
CAUSE: JOB STRESS
IN
IN

PROBLEM: OVERSPENDING
CAUSE: JOB STRESS
PROBLEM: CRANKINESS
CAUSE: JOB STRESS

PROBLEM: EXHAUSTION, DISORGANIZATION, WRINKLES, TOOTH DECAY, ERODING SOCIAL SKILLS, HOSTILITY, FLAB.
CAUSE: JOB STRESS
JOB STRESS
JOB STRESS
JOB STRESS

ON THE BRIGHT SIDE, I BELIEVE I'VE IDENTIFIED A REMARKABLY PRODUCTIVE AREA OF MY CAREER.
IN
IN

IMAGINE A WORLD WHERE WEIGHT DOESN'T MATTER...
YES!...
ONLINE WORLD

IMAGINE SLUMPING ON THE COUCH IN A SWEATSUIT, WITH NO MAKEUP AND HIDEOUS HAIR AND HAVING MILLIONS OF WITTY, ELIGIBLE MEN WAITING TO SAY "HI" TO YOU...
YES! YES!
ONLINE WORLD

IMAGINE TURNING THEM DOWN WITH ONE FLICK OF YOUR BROWNIE-CRUMB-COVERED, UNMANICURED FINGER...
YES! I WANT THAT! YES!!
ONLINE WORLD

LOVE IN THE '90s: GOODBYE, AQUA NET. HELLO, INTERNET.
ONLINE WORLD

OF COURSE THERE ARE MEN ONLINE! MILLIONS OF MEN! SINGLE MEN! BRILLIANT MEN! FASCINATING MEN!
ONLINE TODAY

EMOTIONALLY ACCESSIBLE MEN! MEN WHO CAN TYPE! MEN WHO LOVE TO CHAT INTO THE WEE HOURS!

MEN WHO DON'T LIVE IN THIS STUPID TOWN!
SOLD!
ONLINE TODAY

AACK! VIRTUAL INSULT!
...THIS FROM A MAN WHOSE IDEA OF COMMITMENT IS SHARING HIS SECRET SCREEN NAME WITH A WOMAN IN PERU.

I'D LIKE A BASIC HOME COMPUTER SO I CAN MEET SOME INTERESTING MEN ONLINE.
COMPUTER SUPERSTORE

GREAT! YOU'LL WANT A 75MHz PENTIUM PROCESSOR OR APPLE POWERPC WITH 8MB RAM AND 850 HARD DRIVE...A 28.8Kbps MODEM, V.34 STANDARD, WITH TELEPHONY...A 15-INCH SVGA MONITOR WITH AT LEAST 800-BY-600 RESOLUTION, 16-BIT COLOR, 64-BIT GRAPHICS ACCELERATOR, AND A DOT PITCH OF NO MORE THAN .28mm... OPERATING SYSTEM, ONLINE SOFTWARE, AND, OF COURSE, AN ERGONOMICALLY CORRECT CHAIR!
1GB

WHY NOT JUST SAY "HI" THE NEXT TIME YOU SEE SOMEONE YOU LIKE?
TOO INTIMIDATING.
SUPERSTORE

WHEN I SHOPPED FOR A COMPUTER TEN YEARS AGO, A 5-MEGABYTE HARD DISK WAS BIG ENOUGH TO HANDLE EVERY DOCUMENT I COULD CREATE IN A LIFETIME...
850 MB HD
PENTIUM 75
8 MB RAM
15" FLAT SVGA

...NOW YOU'RE TELLING ME I NEED AN 850-MEGABYTE HARD DISK TO EVEN INSTALL THE PROGRAM TO PRODUCE ONE MEASLY THANK-YOU NOTE?
850 MB HD
PENTIUM 75
8 MB RAM
15" FLAT SVGA

HAH!

THE 1996 MEMORY FIASCO: THE COMPUTERS NEVER HAVE ENOUGH, AND THE CONSUMERS ALWAYS HAVE TOO MUCH.

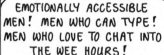

"50 CALORIES PER SERVING" ... SO WHAT? HA, HA! I CAN AFFORD 50 CALORIES!
50
I WORKED HARD TODAY! I DESERVE A 50-CALORIE SNACK! I EARNED A 50-CALORIE REWARD! HAH!
SNACK
50
"15 SERVINGS PER PACKAGE."
50
SNACK
I TOOK MY MIND OFF DRIVING FOR FOUR SECONDS AND HAD A TEN-POUND COLLISION WITH FAT.
Guisewite

THREE THINGS MATTER IN A COMPUTER: **SPEED, SPEED,** AND **SPEED!** 75, 100, EVEN 133 MEGAHERTZ PROCESSORS!

...16MEG OF STREAKING RAM, PUMPED EVEN FASTER BY EDO MEMORY AND/OR A HIGH-SPEED SECONDARY CACHE!! CD-ROM BLASTING AT QUAD-SPEED!! MODEM FLYING AT 28,000 BITS PER SECOND!! IT'S **SPEED! MEGA SPEED!!**

WHY DOES IT NEED TO GO SO FAST?
YOU HAVE TO MAKE UP FOR THE TWO MONTHS YOU'LL WASTE TRYING TO FIGURE OUT WHAT TO BUY!!

OH, FOR CRYING OUT LOUD.
FOUR MONTHS IF YOU START OVER IN ANOTHER STORE BECAUSE EVERYTHING THEY TELL YOU WILL BE TOTALLY DIFFERENT!

1981: WANTED TO MEET SOMEONE NEW, SO ENROLLED IN ADULT ED. COURSE.
COST: $65.00
COOKING FOR TWO

1987: WANTED TO MEET SOMEONE NEW, SO SIGNED UP FOR DATING SERVICE.
COST: $300.00
VIDEO-MATE #47289Q

1990: WANTED TO MEET SOMEONE NEW, SO JOINED A GYM.
COST: $500.00
ELEVATED HEARTRATE

1996: WANTED TO MEET SOMEONE NEW, SO BEGAN SHOPPING FOR COMPUTER, MONITOR, MODEM AND SOFTWARE TO CONNECT TO ONLINE ROMANCE CHAT ROOM.
COST: $2,400.00
PC VS MAC
NET SURF

SOMEDAY MY PRINCE WILL COME, AND WHEN HE DOES, HE'D BETTER BE CARRYING A GREAT BIG BAG OF MONEY.

THE BASIC MULTIMEDIA SYSTEM IS...
I DON'T NEED MULTI-MEDIA. I ONLY WANT MY COMPUTER TO DO TWO THINGS.
MULTIMEDIA

OF COURSE YOU NEED MULTIMEDIA! **EVERYONE** NEEDS MULTIMEDIA!
I NEED A TWO-THINGS SYSTEM! I DO NOT NEED A MULTI-MEDIA SYSTEM!

I WILL **NOT** BE INTIMIDATED INTO BUYING MORE THAN I NEED!! DO I LOOK THAT GULLIBLE?? **DO I LOOK LIKE I WAS BORN YESTERDAY?? HAH!**

IF YOU WERE BORN YESTER-DAY, YOU'D **KNOW** YOU NEEDED MULTIMEDIA.
NOT TO MENTION, YOU'D ALREADY KNOW HOW TO USE IT.

THE SYSTEM I DESCRIBED WILL BE JUST LIKE THIS EXCEPT, OF COURSE, YOUR MONITOR WILL BE DIFFERENT, YOUR KEYBOARD WILL BE DIFFERENT, YOUR MOUSE WILL BE DIFFERENT, YOUR SPEAKERS WILL BE DIFFERENT, YOUR ROM DRIVE WILL BE DIFFERENT, YOUR MODEM WILL BE DIFFERENT, YOUR SPEED WILL BE DIFFERENT, AND YOUR SOFTWARE WILL BE DIFFERENT!

I'M SPENDING A FORTUNE, AND I CAN'T EVEN TRY WHAT I'M BUYING?? ISN'T THERE ANYTHING SIMILAR? ANYTHING SIMILAR AT ALL??

OF COURSE! YOUR PRICE TAG WILL LOOK EXACTLY LIKE THIS EXCEPT THE NUMBERS WILL BE HIGHER!

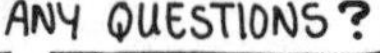

ANY QUESTIONS?

YES. IF COMPUTERS ARE SO FRIENDLY, WHY ARE THEY COVERED WITH MEAN WORDS LIKE "RAM", "GIGABYTE" AND "MEGAHERTZ"??

WHY ARE THE BROCHURES SO ICKY AND INTIMIDATING?? WHY ARE THE STORES SO BORING AND COLD?? WHY ARE THE CATALOGS SO UGLY??!

WHY DOES EVERY AD HAVE 10,000 FOREIGN WORDS IN MINUSCULE TYPE?? AND WHY ISN'T THERE ONE PRETTY SIGN ANYWHERE THAT SAYS IN PLAIN ENGLISH WHAT I NEED??!

THOSE WHO CAN, DO. THOSE WHO CAN'T, ART DIRECT.

DO I WANT A MAC OR DO I WANT A PC?
I THOUGHT A MAC WAS A PC.
MAC PC
MAC VS. PC

A MAC IS A PC, BUT IT'S NOT CALLED A PC BECAUSE IT'S JUST NOT. EXCEPT THE MAC POWERPC, WHICH HAS PC IN ITS NAME, BUT IS STILL REFERRED TO AS A MAC, NOT A PC.
HUH?
MAC PC
MAC VS. PC

FOR CRYING OUT LOUD, CHARLENE! IT'S THE MOST BASIC THING ABOUT COMPUTERS! THERE ARE TWO DISTINCT SYSTEMS! ONE IS MAC AND ONE IS PC!!
OH.

...SO, DO I WANT A MAC, OR DO I WANT A PC?
I THOUGHT A MAC WAS A PC.
MAC PC
MAC VS. PC

NINE HOURS OF STUDYING COMPUTER MAGAZINES, AND WHAT HAVE I LEARNED?? I'M AN IDIOT!!
COMPUTERS

TWELVE HOURS OF SHOPPING IN SEVEN DIFFERENT STORES.. ...WHAT DO I KNOW THAT I DIDN'T KNOW BEFORE?? I'M AN IDIOT!!

TWO WEEKS OF MY LIFE SPENT TRYING TO SORT OUT 45 PEOPLE'S OPINIONS ON WHAT I NEED... WHAT CONCLUSION CAN I DRAW?? I'M AN IDIOT!!

THE NEW CPU'S ARE SO FAST! IT USED TO TAKE MONTHS TO REACH THIS POINT!
COMPUTERS

IF I BUY THIS SYSTEM, WILL YOU PROMISE IT WON'T BE OBSOLETE NEXT WEEK?
NEXT WEEK? ARE YOU KIDDING?? IT WON'T BE OBSOLETE NEXT WEEK!
PRINTER
MODEM
MONITOR
COMPUTER
KEYBOARD

IT'S ALREADY OBSOLETE! IT WAS OBSOLETE BEFORE IT WAS SHIPPED TO THE STORE! THE SYSTEM THAT WILL REPLACE IT THAT HASN'T EVEN BEEN MANUFACTURED YET IS ALREADY OBSOLETE!

"OBSOLETE NEXT WEEK"?? HOO, BOY! THAT'S A GOOD ONE!! THANKS! I NEEDED A CHUCKLE TODAY! !HA HA HOO HA HA!
SALES

...AND THEY SAY THE COMPUTER INDUSTRY HAS NO SENSE OF HUMOR.

VALENTINE PLANNING, 1988:

I WANT TO BE READY IN CASE IRVING SURPRISES ME WITH A ROMANTIC DINNER ABOARD A YACHT AND HAS ARRANGED FOR A DOVE TO SWOOP DOWN WITH A DIAMOND RING IN ITS BEAK.

Nail Boutique

VALENTINE PLANNING, 1992:

I WANT TO BE READY IN CASE THE MAN WHO GLANCED AT ME AT THE STOPLIGHT IN JANUARY HAS SPENT THE LAST MONTH SEARCHING FOR ME AND IS HAVING TWO DOZEN ROSES DELIVERED TO MY HOME BY HIS PRIVATE CHAUFFEUR!

Housewares

VALENTINE PLANNING, 1996:

I WANT TO BE READY IN CASE I DECIDE ON A COMPUTER, SET IT UP, CONNECT TO THE INTERNET, SCAN THROUGH 20 MILLION POTENTIAL HEARTTHROBS AND FALL IN LOVE WITH ONE BY WEDNESDAY!

THE ONLY THING I'M NEVER PREPARED FOR IS REALITY.
WHY BOTHER? THERE'S NOTHING TO SHOP FOR.

HAVE YOU QUIT AUTOMATICALLY REJECTING MEN WHO DON'T MEET EVERY REQUIREMENT ON YOUR LIST?
NO.
Tissues
VALENTINE COUNSELOR

HAVE YOU DONE ANYTHING NEW TO MEET MEN?
NO.
HAVE YOU CHANGED YOUR ESSENTIAL BEHAVIOR PATTERN TOWARD MEN IN ANY REAL WAY SINCE JUNIOR HIGH?
NO.

WHAT SENTIMENT WOULD YOU LIKE YOUR CARD TO EXPRESS?
IT'S ALL THEIR FAULT!!
Tissues
VALENTINE COUNSELOR

NOTHING LIKE VALENTINE'S WEEK TO INSPIRE THE TRADITIONALIST IN US ALL.
TINES
Be Mine

THE ANNUAL VALENTINE'S NIGHT EMOTIONAL EVALUATION

IS THERE SOMEONE WHO LOVES ME COMPLETELY?... YES.

IS THERE SOMEONE WHO ACCEPTS ME AS I AM?.... YES.
IS THERE SOMEONE I CAN POUR MY HEART OUT TO WHO RESPONDS BY KISSING AND BEGGING FOR MORE?...YES!

KISS

..sigh..
HOW MUCH BETTER DOES SHE THINK IT'S GOING TO GET?
diet

REMEMBER "CATHY VS. IRVING", 1991?? YOU STOMPED INTO HIS OFFICE AND DUMPED A TWO-POUND BOX OF EMPTY CHOCOLATE WRAPPERS ON HIS DESK!!

HA, HA! HOW ABOUT "CHARLENE VS. FRANKIE," 1982?? YOU SPENT A MONTH EMBROIDERING "I LOVE YOU" ONTO PILLOWCASES, AND HE GAVE YOU A DUSTBUSTER!!
HOO, HA! 1993! MARCIA CHASED TED AROUND THE ALL-NIGHT DRIVING RANGE IN A SLINKY RED DRESS WAVING HIS FIVE-IRON OVER HER HEAD!
HA, HA! 1986! BRENDA THREW HER NEW VALENTINE PLAQUE REMOVER THROUGH BOB'S NEW WINDSHIELD!

MEN REMEMBER FOOTBALL BLOOPERS. WOMEN REMEMBER VALENTINE BLUNDERS.

I'M GOING TO LOSE 20 POUNDS, MOM!
AND I'M GOING TO DO A POWER WALK EVERY MORNING!

I'M GOING TO BUDGET EVERY CENT I SPEND!
AND I'M GOING TO ORGANIZE THE BASEMENT!
I'M GOING TO MEET MY MATE IN CYBERSPACE!
AND I WILL BE A SIZE SIX FOR THE WEDDING!

AT LAST. A PERFECT MOTHER-DAUGHTER MOMENT.

I KNEW IT WAS THE CHOCOLATE TALKING... AND SHE KNEW IT WAS THE CHOCOLATE LISTENING.

I RESEARCHED COMPUTERS FOR A MONTH AND THEN TOOK A WEEK OFF TO CLEAR MY HEAD SO I COULD MAKE AN INTELLIGENT DECISION...
POWER PC

.....AND NOW MY HEAD IS CLEAR. MY BRAIN IS COMPLETELY BLANK!! I DON'T REMEMBER ANYTHING! I CAN'T EVEN UNDERSTAND MY OWN NOTES!!
POWER PC

WHAT IS ALL THIS JUNK?! WHAT DO THESE NUMBERS MEAN?? I'VE FORGOTTEN EVERYTHING! I'M BACK TO ZERO! I REMEMBER NOTHING AT ALL!!!

AACK! WHAT PRICE DILIGENCE?!
WOULDN'T MATTER. THERE HAVE BEEN 10,000 PRICE CHANGES AND 7,200 NEW PRODUCTS SINCE YOU WERE HERE LAST.

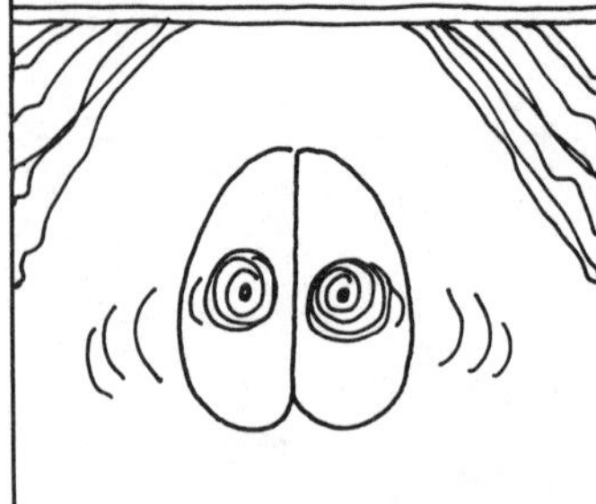
EYES BUGGY FROM SPENDING NINE HOURS TRYING TO DECIPHER TEN PEOPLE'S OPINIONS ON WHETHER I NEED 8 OR 16 MEGS OF RAM.

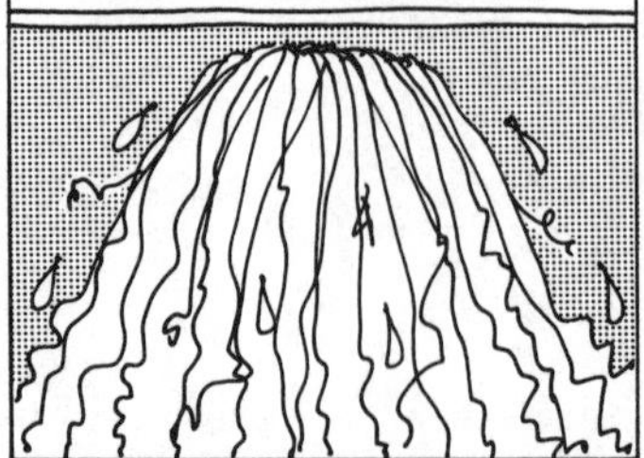
HAIR SWEATY AND ICKY FROM ARGUING WITH A SALESPERSON OVER WHY HE DIDN'T MENTION THE ESSENTIAL $500 MONITOR WASN'T INCLUDED IN THE "COMPLETE PACKAGE PRICE".

CLOTHES SMUDGED AND WADDED UP FROM HAULING 46 NEWSPAPER AD COST COMPARISONS ON THE 600dpi INK JET PRINTER TO FOURTEEN SEPARATE STORES.

I HAVEN'T EVEN BOUGHT THE COMPUTER YET, AND I'VE ALREADY TURNED INTO A NERD.

YOU LIVED YOUR WHOLE LIFE PREPARING TO BE SOMEONE'S VALENTINE, AND NO ONE PICKED YOU.
1/2 OFF
SALE

YOU TRIED TO FIT IN BY LOOKING LIKE A CLONE, AND THEN YOU GOT PASSED OVER BECAUSE NO ONE NOTICED YOU WERE SPECIAL.

I KNOW THAT WHAT YOU HAVE INSIDE IS STILL JUST AS RICH AND VALUABLE!! I KNOW HOW MUCH YOU HAVE TO GIVE! I VOW TO LOOK PAST THE LABEL SOCIETY HAS STUCK ON YOU AND SAVOUR EVERY MOMENT OF OUR TIME TOGETHER!!!
SALE
SALE

GOODBYE, EMPTY CALORIES. HELLO, EMPATHY CALORIES.
SALE
Guisewite

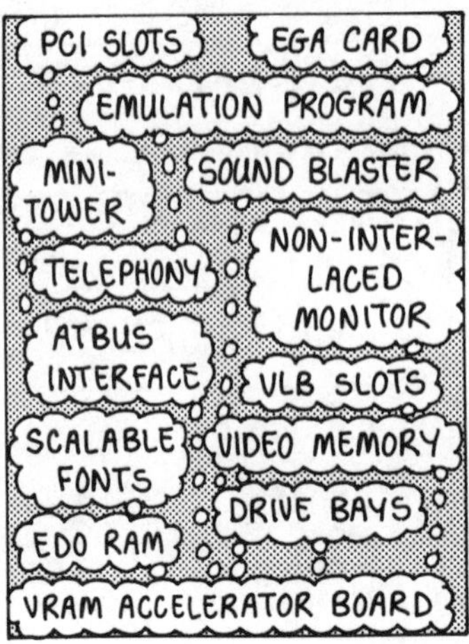

I SPENT TWO HOURS ON THE PHONE WITH THE SOFTWARE HOTLINE MAN... TWO HOURS WITH THE MODEM TROUBLE-SHOOTER MAN... AND THREE HOURS WITH THE "I-JUST-SPENT-$2000-AND-I-CAN'T GET-THE-STUPID-MACHINE-TO-TURN-ON" MAN!!